D0623150

Manual of Smoking Cessation

Manual of Smoking Cessation

A guide for counsellors and practitioners

Andy McEwen
Peter Hajek
Hayden McRobbie
Robert West

Addiction
Press

Blackwell Publishing Ltd editorial offices:
Blackwell Publishing Ltd, 9600 Garsington Road, Oxford OX4 2DQ, UK
Tel: +44 (0)1865 776868
Blackwell Publishing Inc., 350 Main Street, Malden, MA 02148-5020, USA
Tel: +1 781 388 8250
Blackwell Publishing Asia Pty Ltd, 550 Swanston Street, Carlton, Victoria 3053, Australia
Tel: +61 (0)3 8359 1011

First published 2006 by Blackwell Publishing Ltd

ISBN-10: 1-4051-3337-6
ISBN-13: 978-1-4051-3337-1

Library of Congress Cataloging-in-Publication Data

Manual of smoking cessation : a guide for counsellors and practitioners /
Andy McEwen . . . [et al.].
p. cm.
Includes bibliographical references and index.
ISBN-13: 978-1-4051-3337-1 (pbk. : alk. paper)
ISBN-10: 1-4051-3337-6 (pbk. : alk. paper) 1. Smoking cessation–Handbooks, manuals, etc. 2. Cigarette smokers–Rehabilitation–Handbooks, manuals, etc. 3. Nicotine addiction–Treatment–Handbooks, manuals, etc. I. McEwen, Andy.

RC567.M36 2006
616.86′506–dc22
2005035902

A catalogue record for this title is available from the British Library

Set in 10.5/13 pt Legacy Sans
by Graphicraft Typesetters Ltd
Printed and bound in Spain
by GraphyCems, Navarra

The publisher's policy is to use permanent paper from mills that operate a sustainable forestry policy, and which has been manufactured from pulp processed using acid-free and elementary chlorine-free practices. Furthermore, the publisher ensures that the text paper and cover board used have met acceptable environmental accreditation standards.

For further information on Blackwell Publishing, visit our website:
www.blackwellpublishing.com

Contents

About the authors

Andy McEwen is Senior Research Nurse at the Cancer Research UK Health Behaviour Unit at University College London. His current research includes surveys of smokers and health professionals, pharmacokinetic studies on nicotine delivery systems and clinical trials of behavioural treatments. He also retains an interest in nursing research. In 1997, he began his clinical and academic career in smoking cessation with Robert West. In 2003, he took up his current post and is Director of the Smoking Cessation Services Research Network (SCSRN) and Programme Director of the UK National Smoking Cessation Conference (UKNSCC).

Peter Hajek is Professor of Clinical Psychology, Head of Psychology, and Director of Tobacco Dependence Research Unit at Bart's and the London, Queen Mary's School of Medicine and Dentistry, University of London. His research is concerned primarily with understanding smoking behaviour and developing and evaluating smoking cessation treatments. He has authored or co-authored over 200 publications, holds various academic and editorial appointments and had input into the UK Government's initiative to establish smoking cessation services. His unit is involved in examining both behavioural and pharmacological interventions, and in offering treatment to dependent smokers who seek help.

Dr Hayden McRobbie is a Research Fellow at the Clinical Trials Research Unit, University of Auckland, New Zealand, where he specialises in smoking cessation research and treatment. He studied medicine at the University of Otago and after several years in clinical medicine he moved to London to work with Professor Peter Hajek. He worked on a large number of projects and clinical trials looking at ways to help people stop smoking, as well as pharmacological and behavioural methods that alleviate the symptoms of tobacco withdrawal. In New Zealand, Hayden continues his research into treatment to help people stop smoking and retains close links with the UK, where he is a visiting lecturer at Bart's and the London, Queen Mary's School of Medicine and Dentistry and Programme Director of the UK National Smoking Cessation Conference.

Robert West is Director of Tobacco Studies at the Cancer Research UK Health Behaviour Unit at University College London. He has been researching tobacco and nicotine dependence since 1982 and has published more than 250 scientific works. His research involves surveys of smoking patterns, clinical trials of aids to smoking cessation and laboratory studies of nicotine withdrawal symptoms. He is co-author of the English National Smoking Cessation Guidelines that provided the blueprint for the English Stop Smoking Services and is also Editor-in-Chief of the journal *Addiction*.

Acknowledgements

All the authors would like to thank their host institutions for their support in the writing of this manual: University College London (Andy McEwen and Robert West), Bart's and the London, Queen Mary's School of Medicine and Dentistry (Peter Hajek) and the University of Auckland (Hayden McRobbie).

We would also like to thank all at Blackwell Publishing for their help and support, especially Caroline Connelly and Amy Brown.

This manual would not have been possible if it were not for the invaluable support of Cancer Research UK.

Statements of professional interest

Andy McEwen has received travel funding and honorariums from manufacturers of smoking cessation products. He also receives payment for providing training to smoking cessation specialists and receives royalties from books on smoking cessation. He is a director of the UK National Smoking Cessation Conference (UKNSCC) and the director of the Smoking Cessation Services Research Network (SCSRN).

Peter Hajek undertakes consultancy for and has received fees, research funds and travel expenses from companies developing and manufacturing smoking cessation products. He also receives payment for providing training to smoking cessation specialists. He is a director of Smoking Cessation Training and Research Programme.

Hayden McRobbie has received hospitality and contributions towards conference attendance from the manufacturers of smoking cessation medications. He is also a director of the UK National Smoking Cessation Conference (UKNSCC).

Robert West undertakes consultancy for and has received fees, research funds and travel expenses from companies developing and manufacturing smoking cessation products. He also receives payment for helping with training smoking cessation specialists and receives royalties from books on smoking.

Foreword

Gay Sutherland
Tobacco Research Unit, Institute of Psychiatry

The smoking cessation field has undergone rapid growth over the last few years and there is now an extensive group of health care professionals from many different backgrounds who have become involved in this area. Smoking cessation is an important issue and there is ever increasing pressure to treat more smokers more effectively. New advances in service development and in research into treating smokers are now regularly being reported in addition to the wealth of experience being gained by smoking cessation services and clinicians from around the UK. The *Manual of Smoking Cessation: A guide for counsellors and practitioners* expertly synthesises the evidence base with current good practice to produce detailed advice on how best to help smokers to quit.

The *Manual* conveys essential background information on smoking prevalence and patterns, health risks of smoking, nicotine dependence and the tobacco withdrawal syndrome in a clear and concise manner. What really sets this book apart however is the way that the authors have managed to provide expert, comprehensive but comprehensible guidance for those treating smokers. This clear guidance on what to do and say to smokers wanting to stop is supplemented by the clever use of suggested phrases and frequently asked questions throughout the text. The result is not merely another text book; the *Manual* is exactly what it says in the title, it is *A guide for counsellors and practitioners*.

I am delighted to be able to introduce the *Manual of Smoking Cessation: A guide for counsellors and practitioners*. This is a much needed and eagerly awaited publication which provides essential knowledge and guidance for those involved in smoking cessation. It is an indispensable guide, both for those working as specialist smoking cessation counsellors and for practitioners who would like to do a little more for their smoking patients.

Introduction

The *Manual of Smoking Cessation* provides the essential knowledge required if you are involved in helping smokers to stop.

The manual aims to provide facts, figures, suggested interventions and sources of further information to assist you in providing evidence-based treatment for smokers wishing to stop. **This manual covers** the **core content areas** and **key learning outcomes** described in the **Standard for training in smoking cessation treatments** published by the Health Development Agency in 2003.

The book is divided into two parts and six chapters:

Part One: Essential Information

- Chapter 1 'Smoking demographics' looks at the **prevalence** and **patterns** of smoking and smoking cessation.
- Chapter 2 'The health risks of smoking and the benefits of stopping'.

Part Two: Practical Advice

- Chapter 3 'Brief interventions' gives information to help you assess and record smoking status, **advise smokers to stop** and assess their interest in quitting. This chapter also covers **nicotine dependence**, **compensatory smoking** and **onward referral**.
- Chapter 4 'Intensive one-to-one support' gives you the knowledge needed to provide intensive one-to-one behavioural support. It covers **assessing nicotine dependence** and **motivation to quit**, plus **smoking cessation treatments**, their outcomes and **medications** available to help with stopping smoking.
- Chapter 5 'Telephone counselling'.

- Chapter 6 'Group interventions' provides information needed to carry out group interventions with smokers. This chapter covers the **content of group treatment**, the means of **providing it** and **managing group processes.**

Examples of what to say to clients

Throughout the manual there are boxes like this one that make suggestions about what to say during smoking cessation interventions with clients.

Multiple choice questions

Question 1: Placed at the end of most chapters throughout the manual to:

- **a** Help with learning
- **b** Remind reader of important points
- **c** Test knowledge
- **d** Act as a revision aid
- **e** Be a resource for training purposes

FAQs (frequently asked questions)

Why are these included throughout the manual?

To inform the reader of common questions that they are likely to face from smokers and to suggest best ways of responding.

See Appendix 5.

This manual is not intended as a substitute for obtaining training and experience in smoking cessation. It is designed to complement any training that you receive and to encourage you to maximise the experience that you can gain from working with smokers wanting to stop.

Part One:
Essential Information

Chapter 1
Smoking demographics

This chapter summarises smoking prevalence and patterns as functions of age, gender, ethnic origin and social class. It also looks at patterns of smoking cessation.

1.1 Smoking patterns

1.1.1 Smoking prevalence

Since the 1970s there has been a steady decline in smoking in the UK, although this levelled off during the 1990s (Figure 1.1) and is currently falling by 0.4% per year (Jarvis, 2003). In 2003, **26%** of the

Figure 1.1 Smoking prevalence in the UK since 1974.

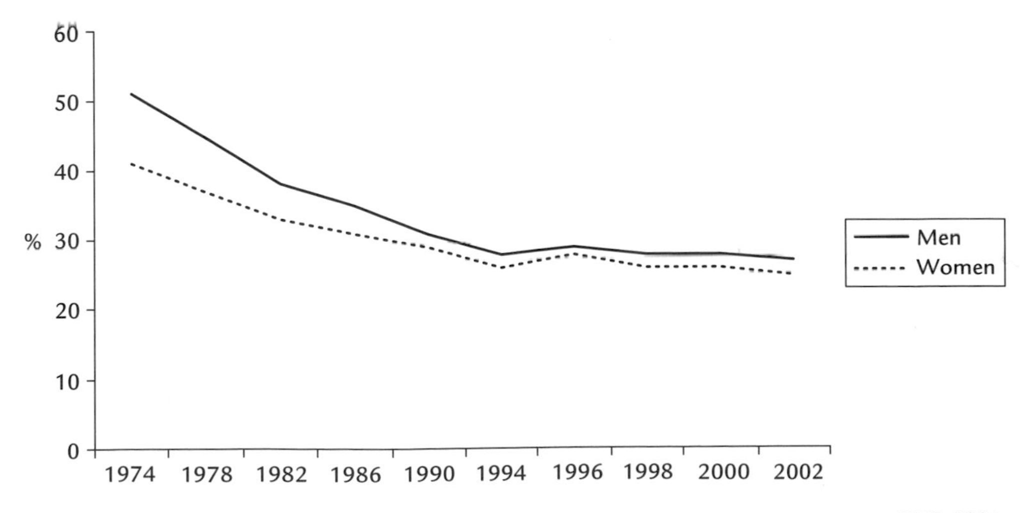

ONS, 2004.

UK adult population smoked cigarettes: approximately **12.5 million people** (NatCen, 2004). Within the UK there is considerable **variation in smoking** prevalence according to **gender**, **age**, **socio-economic status** and **ethnicity**.

In 2003, **27%** of **men** and **24%** of **women smoked cigarettes** (NatCen, 2004). The gender gap is widened slightly if other tobacco products are taken into consideration; a further 2% of adult men smoke pipes in the UK and 4% smoke cigars (ONS, 2004). Over the past ten years in the UK there has been an increasing trend towards smoking hand-rolled cigarettes (West & McEwen, 1999). In 2002, **30%** of **male smokers** and **11%** of **female smokers** reported **smoking hand-rolled cigarettes** (NatCen, 2004); 9% of male and female smokers report using both hand-rolled and manufactured cigarettes (ONS, 2004).

Is the tobacco used for roll-up cigarettes healthier because it has fewer additives?

No, smoke from rolling tobacco still contains tar and carbon monoxide. Just like cigarettes, this tobacco also has substances added to it to make the smoke less of an irritant and taste sweeter. It is not a healthier, more natural alternative.

The commonly held view that women in Britain are more likely to smoke than men is only true in younger people under 16 years of age and, marginally so, for those aged over 65 (Figure 1.2).

Figure 1.2 Smoking prevalence by age group, UK 2003.

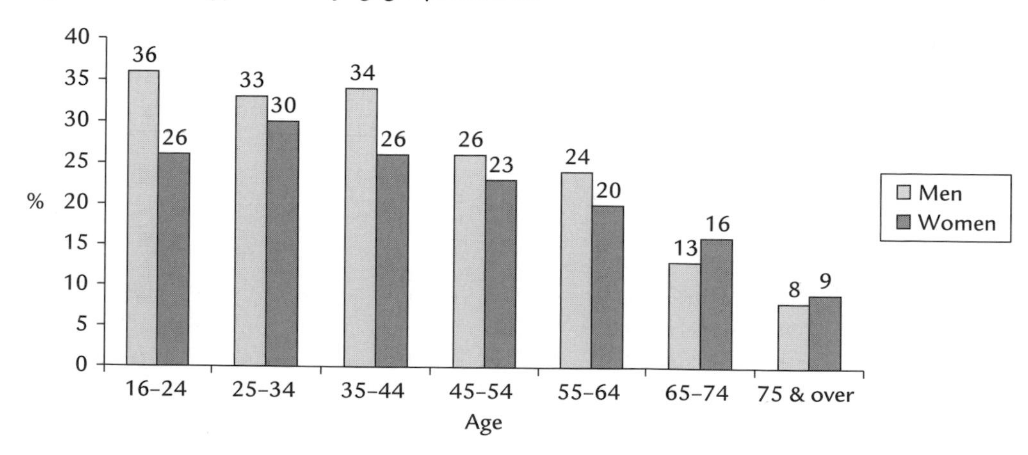

Adapted from ONS, 2004.

There is generally a **lower level** of **cigarette smoking** among **minority ethnic groups** than among the UK population as a whole. In 1996, 29% of the UK adult population smoked cigarettes (ONS, 1997); this compared with 28% of Bangladeshis, 27% of African-Caribbeans, 15% of Pakistanis and 10% of Indians (McEwen & West, 1999). Whilst these figures suggest that smoking is slightly less of a risk factor for African-Caribbean and Bangladeshi communities, and much less of a risk factor for Indians and Pakistanis overall, the analysis by gender shows a different picture (Figure 1.3).

Figure 1.3 Regular smokers by gender in different ethnic groups, UK 1996.

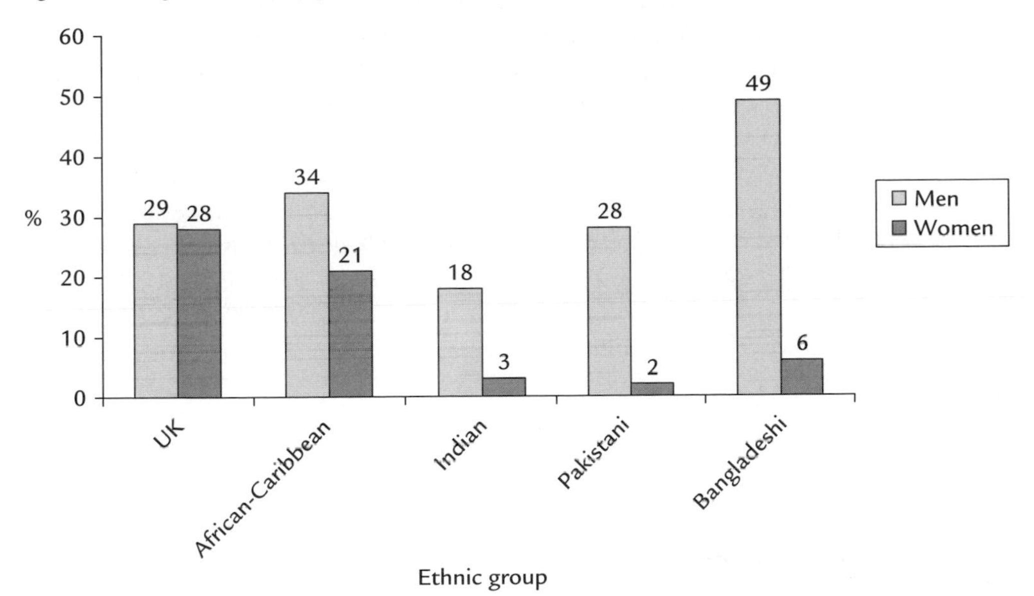

McEwen & West, 1999.

I heard that there are more women who smoke than men – is this true?

In the UK slightly more men than women smoke (27% versus 24%) and a further 6% of men smoke cigars or pipes. There are more girls than boys under 16 who smoke, but by their twenties the situation is reversed.

Do women find it harder to stop smoking than men?

Some researchers have proposed that women find it more difficult to quit, but this does not seem to be the case and they have as good a chance of quitting as men. For the best chance of stopping smoking smokers should get treatment from their local NHS Stop Smoking Service.

Age also has an impact on smoking prevalence within these ethnic groups. Among male smokers of **African-Caribbean**, **Indian** and **Pakistani** origin the **highest prevalence** is found between the ages of **30** and **49**; for **Bangladeshis** it is between **50** and **74**, where 70% are regular cigarette smokers (McEwen & West, 1999). Smokers of Bangladeshi origin also provide the exception to the age-related decrease in prevalence found with African-Caribbean, Indian and Pakistani women, although it remains relatively low at 14% (McEwen & West, 1999).

The prevalence of cigarette **smoking is higher** among the **socio-economically disadvantaged**: among men, 20% of those in managerial and professional households smoke, compared with 35% in households with semi-routine and routine occupations. For women, the equivalent figures are 18% and 32% (NatCen, 2004). Figure 1.4 shows the social gradient of smoking prevalence in the UK. **Educational achievement** is also associated with **smoking prevalence**. In fact, low educational achievement is a risk factor for smoking in children (Barton, 1998). **Smoking** prevalence in the UK also **varies according to region**: it is highest in the north west region (30%) and lowest in the south and west region (25%) (Department of Health, 1998).

Figure 1.4 Prevalence of cigarette smoking among adults by social class and sex, UK 2002.

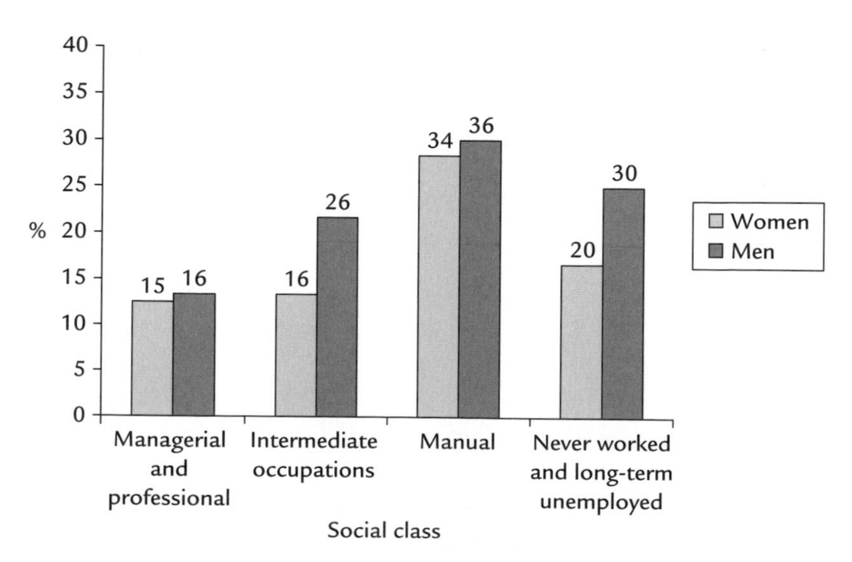

Office for National Statistics, 2004.

1.1.2 Smoking consumption

Males smoke an average of **14.5 cigarettes a day**, compared with **13.3 smoked by women** (NatCen, 2004); 37% of male and 25% of female smokers smoked 20 cigarettes or more per day in 2001 (Lader & Meltzer, 2003). Men tend to smoke higher tar cigarettes than women; almost two-thirds (62%) of male smokers smoke high tar cigarettes compared with 52% of female smokers (ONS, 1997). A recent survey suggests that men may be more dependent on cigarettes than women, as determined by the proportion who smoke within 30 minutes of waking: **40% of female smokers** reported smoking their **first cigarette within 30 minutes of waking**, compared with **44% of male smokers** (Lader & Meltzer, 2003).

1.1.3 Exposure to environmental tobacco smoke

Non-smokers are more sensitive to exhaled smoke than smokers, and sidestream smoke is more toxic, for the same concentration, than mainstream smoke (Glantz & Parmley, 1995). Exposure to cigarette smoke is not uncommon among the general population of non-smokers and they are at risk at home, at work, when socialising and in public places.

All that fear of other people's smoke seems exaggerated. Surely having some smoke in the air cannot do much damage can it?

It is scientifically proven that exposure to second-hand smoke is associated with increased risk of cot death, coronary heart disease and even lung cancer. Furthermore, approximately 11 000 people die each year in the UK as a result of second-hand smoke.

1.1.4 Beliefs about smoking

Table 1.1 shows the main reasons why people say that they smoke; these reasons may also contribute to returning to smoking at any time.

Table 1.1 Common self-reported reasons for smoking.

Reason for smoking	Comment
Stress relief	Giving up smoking is stressful. But all the evidence shows that ex-smokers and non-smokers are less stressed than smokers. If smokers stop smoking and stay stopped then they will suffer less from stress and anxiety.
Socialising	It is getting harder to smoke in public places and will become harder still in the future. When smokers have stopped smoking then those places where there are lots of smokers about will be a high risk situation for returning back to smoking.
Boredom	Smoking can kill time, but unfortunately it can kill the smoker as well. When people have stopped smoking they will have time for those hobbies and jobs that they didn't before.
Concentration aid	If a cigarette improves concentration it is probably only because concentration levels are low in the first place because the smoker hasn't had a cigarette for a while and is in nicotine withdrawal.
Alertness	Nicotine is a mild stimulant, but it is unlikely that smokers will notice any real effect. As with concentration, if a cigarette improves alertness it is probably only because the smoker was feeling lethargic because they hadn't had a cigarette for a while.
Weight control	Nicotine increases metabolic rate (so that more calories are 'burned up') and slightly reduces appetite. When smokers stop smoking they can expect to put on weight (see Chapter 4—4.4 Behavioural support – withdrawal oriented treatment, 4.4.1 Preparation).
Enjoyment	Most smokers freely admit that they don't enjoy every cigarette that they smoke; in fact they do not enjoy most of the cigarettes that they smoke. Cigarette smoking tends to become all about avoiding nicotine withdrawals and habit, and less about enjoyment.

1.2 Smoking cessation

Many smokers are uncomfortable with their continued smoking and report a variety of reasons for why they would like to stop (see Box 1.1). A majority of cigarette smokers, **70%**, report that they **would like to stop smoking** (ONS, 2004), and indeed they attempt to stop many times. Results from a national survey of smokers and ex-smokers revealed that in a 12-month period **32%** of smokers had **made a quit attempt** (West & McEwen, 1999) and **33%** had **tried to cut down**

Box 1.1 Common reasons for wanting to stop smoking.

Worries about future health	Smoking restrictions
Cost of smoking	Pressure from family
Current health	Doctor's advice

(ONS, 2004). However, attempts to stop smoking and the chances of success of these attempts are not homogeneous among smokers.

Cessation rates are **lower** in more **deprived socio-economic** groups (Hymowitz et al., 1997); this appears to reflect both attempts to stop (ONS, 2004) and the success of those attempts. There is some evidence that women find it harder to stop than men, but other studies have failed to find this effect. It appears that younger smokers are more likely to make a quit attempt but older smokers may be more likely to be successful in attempts to stop smoking (Hatziandreu et al., 1990). Smokers from minority ethnic groups are as ready to stop smoking as their counterparts in the UK population as a whole, but **quit attempts** are **far less common** among **African-Caribbean**, **Indian**, **Pakistani** and **Bangladeshi** smokers (McEwen & West, 1999).

The chances of **success of quit attempts** are **lower** in **those who live with smokers versus non-smokers**, and **those who live alone versus with a partner** (ONS, 1997). In general, social support has been shown in some studies to be linked with success of attempts to stop (Lennox & Taylor, 1994). Conversely, spending **more time in the company of smokers** appears to be related to **lower success rates** in quit attempts (Richmond et al., 1993). Having managed to go for **a long time without smoking** in recent years has been shown to be **related to success of attempts to stop** (Farkas et al., 1996). It has also been suggested that having children at home may affect the desire to stop and success at stopping. In 2002, smokers with children under 16 in the house were more likely to have tried to give up smoking (84%) than those without children in the household (75%) (ONS, 2004).

Why should smokers go to Stop Smoking Services to quit smoking?

There are a lot of smokers who successfully stop smoking without any help. However, this method gives the lowest chance of stopping. By using the treatment offered by Stop Smoking Services, which combines support with the use of medication, smokers are much more likely to quit than going it alone.

As one would expect, stated intentions to stop and desire to stop are related to subsequent quit attempts (Borland et al., 1991). Furthermore, **attempts to stop smoking** are a function of the **perceived adverse effects of smoking**, as well as the **perceived benefits of stopping smoking** (Borland et al., 1991). There is also some evidence that people who start smoking at a younger age are less likely to give up (Chen & Millar, 1998). The **amount** of cigarettes **smoked** has consistently been shown to **predict failure** of attempts to stop smoking (Farkas et al., 1996), **as have** questionnaire measures of **dependence** (Richmond et al., 1993).

The large majority of quit attempts take place without the aid of medication and without professional support (West & McEwen, 1999). In such circumstances the long-term (at least 12 months) continuous abstinence rate is 3–5% (Hughes et al., 2004).

1.3 Sources for updating prevalence statistics

Office for National Statistics (ONS): http://www.statistics.gov.uk

Action on Smoking and Health (ASH): http://www.ash.org.uk

1.4 Multiple choice questions

Question 1: What percentage of the UK adult population smoke?

- a 70%
- b 13%
- c 26%
- d 30%
- e 24%

Question 2: Regarding smoking in the UK, which of the following statements is FALSE?

- a More men smoke than women
- b Recently there has been a decrease in smoking hand-rolled cigarettes
- c UK smoking prevalence is currently falling by 0.4% per year
- d Approximately 12.5 million adults smoke
- e There is variation in smoking prevalence among ethnic groups

Question 3: Regarding smoking prevalence and ethnicity, which of the following statements is FALSE?

a Sex differences in Asian smokers are larger than among white British smokers

b The highest smoking prevalence within the Bangladeshi population is in the 50–74 age group

c Bangladeshis show a similar age-related decline in smoking prevalence to other ethnic minority groups

d Smoking prevalence is higher in Bangladeshi men than Indian men

e Smoking prevalence is higher in African-Caribbean than Asian women

Question 4: Regarding cigarette consumption, which of the following statements is TRUE?

a Men smoke five more cigarettes per day, on average, than women

b 61% of men smoke 20 cigarettes per day

c Men are more likely to smoke high tar cigarettes than women

d Men may be more dependent on cigarettes than women

e 62% of female smokers smoke high tar cigarettes

Question 5: Regarding smoking and socio-economic group, which of the following statements is FALSE?

a Among men, smoking prevalence is lowest in those who have professional or managerial jobs

b More women than men in manual jobs smoke

c Overall, smoking prevalence is higher in manual groups

d Prevalence is lower in those who have never worked and long-term unemployed, than manual workers

e Smoking prevalence is almost equal among men and women in professional jobs

Question 6: Regarding exposure to environmental tobacco smoke, which of the following statements is TRUE?

a Sidestream smoke is less toxic, for the same concentration, than mainstream smoke

b Second-hand smoke is linked to ear infections in children

c People exposed to their partners' second-hand smoke are at no risk

d Second-hand smoke has not been linked to cardiovascular disease

e Non-smokers are equally as sensitive to exhaled smoke as smokers

Question 7: Regarding beliefs about smoking, which of the following statements is FALSE?

a Many smokers say they smoke for stress relief

b Stress levels generally increase when smokers stop

c Weight control is a reason that some smokers give for continuing to smoke

d Smokers weigh less, on average, than non-smokers

e Smokers admit that they don't enjoy every cigarette

Question 8: What percentage of smokers in the UK report that they would like to stop smoking?

a 100%

b 70%

c 66%

d 42%

e 23%

Question 9: What percentage of UK smokers make a quit attempt each year?

a 70%

b 61%

c 50%

d 32%

e 23%

Question 10: Regarding cessation rates, which of the following statements is TRUE?

a Cessation rates are higher in older smokers

b Cessation rates are higher in smokers from lower socio-economic groups

c Evidence confirms that cessation rates are lower in women compared to men

d Cessation rates are higher in those who live with smokers

e Cessation rates have little to do with nicotine dependence

Question 11: Which of the following is not a predictor of stopping smoking?

a Living with a smoker

b Living alone

c Spending time in the company of smokers

d Having managed to go a long time without smoking in the past

e Gender

Question 12: Regarding attempts to stop smoking, which of the following statements is FALSE?

a Attempts to stop are a function of the perceived risks of smoking

b Attempts to stop are a function of the perceived benefits of stopping

c Most attempts to stop are made with the aid of medication

d Attempts to stop are more likely following brief advice from a GP

e Relatively few attempts to stop are made with the aid of Stop Smoking Services

References

Barton, J. (1998). *Young Teenagers and Smoking in 1997*. London: Health Education Authority.

Borland, R., Owen, N. & Hocking, B. (1991). Changes in smoking behaviour after a total workplace smoking ban. *Australian Journal of Public Health, 15* (2), 130–134.

Chen, J. & Millar, W.J. (1998). Age of smoking initiation: implications for quitting. *Health Report, 9* (4), 39–46.

Cook, D.G. & Strachan, D.P. (1997). Health effects of passive smoking. 3. Parental smoking and prevalence of respiratory symptoms and asthma in schoolage children. *Thorax, 52* (12), 1081–1094.

Department of Health (1998). *Smoking Kills: A White Paper on Tobacco*. London: The Stationery Office.

Farkas, A.J., Pierce, J.P., Zhu, S.H., Rosbrook, B., Gilpin, E.A., Berry, C., et al. (1996). Addiction versus stages of change models in predicting smoking cessation. *Addiction, 91* (9), 1271–1280; discussion 1281–1292.

Glantz, S. & Parmley, W. (1995). Passive smoking and heart disease. Mechanisms and risk. *Journal of American Medical Association, 273* (13), 1047–1053.

Hatziandreu, E.J., Pierce, J.P., Lefkopoulou, M., Fiore, M.C., Mills, S.L., Novotny, T.E., et al. (1990). Quitting smoking in the United States in 1986. *Journal of National Cancer Institute, 82* (17), 1402–1406.

Hughes, J.R., Keely, J. & Naud, S. (2004). Shape of the relapse curve and long-term abstinence among untreated smokers. *Addiction, 99* (1), 29–38.

Hymowitz, N., Cummings, K.M., Hyland, A., Lynn, W.R., Pechacek, T.F. & Hartwell, T.D. (1997). Predictors of smoking cessation in a cohort of adult smokers followed for five years. *Tobacco Control, 6* (Suppl. 2), S57–62.

Jarvis, M.J. (2003). Monitoring cigarette smoking prevalence in Britain in a timely fashion. *Addiction, 98* (11), 1569–1574.

Lader, D. & Meltzer, H. (2003). *Smoking Related Attitudes and Behaviour, 2002*. London: Office of National Statistics.

Lennox, A.S. & Taylor, R.J. (1994). Factors associated with outcome in unaided smoking cessation, and a comparison of those who have never tried to stop with those who have. *British Journal of General Practice, 44* (383), 245–250.

Lennox, A., Bain, N., Taylor, R., McKie, L., Donnan, P. & Groves, J. (1998). Stages of change training for opportunistic smoking intervention by the primary health care team. Part I: randomised controlled trial of the effect of training on patient smoking outcomes and health professional behaviour as recalled by patients. *Health Education Journal, 57*, 140–149.

McEwen, A. & West, R. (1999). Tobacco use amongst black and minority ethnic groups in England. In: *Black and Minority Ethnic Groups and Tobacco Use in England. A Practical Resource for Health Professionals*. London: Health Education Agency.

NatCen (2004). *Health Survey for England 2003 – latest trends*. London: National Centre for Social Research. www.dh.gov.uk/assetRoot/04/09/89/14/04098914.pdf

Office for National Statistics (1997). *Living in Britain: Results from the 1996 General Household Survey*. London: The Stationery Office.

Office for National Statistics (2004). *Living in Britain – the 2002 General Household survey*. London: Office for National Statistics.

Richmond, R.L., Kehoe, L.A. & Webster, I.W. (1993). Multivariate models for predicting abstention following intervention to stop smoking by general practitioners. *Addiction*, *88* (8), 1127–1135.

West, R. & McEwen, A. (1999). *Sex and Smoking: Comparisons between Male and Female Smokers*. London: No Smoking Day.

Chapter 2

The health risks of smoking and the benefits of stopping

The causal link between **smoking** and **increased morbidity** and **mortality** is now firmly established (USDHHS, 2004). Importantly, there is strong evidence that by **stopping smoking**, however late in life, smokers can **reduce** their **risk of premature death** (Doll et al., 2004) and can **improve** their current and future **health** (Royal College of Physicians, 2000).

Approximately **4000 chemical** compounds have been identified in cigarette smoke, of which **over 40 are known to cause cancer**. There are three important components of cigarette smoke:

- **Nicotine** is the drug in cigarettes which is **addictive** (it is what keeps smokers smoking), but it does not cause cancer and has, at most, a small effect on risk of cardiovascular disease.
- **Tar** is the name given to all the other chemicals in the smoke particles, and it is these that are linked to **cancer**, **lung disease**, **heart disease** and the **other diseases caused by smoking**.
- **Carbon monoxide** is a gas inhaled by smokers from cigarettes; it is linked to **heart disease** and has **adverse effects in pregnancy**.

2.1 Smoking mortality

In the UK, cigarette smoking is responsible for approximately **106 000 deaths per year** – more than 2000 per week, 300 per day, 12 per hour (Twigg et al., 2004).

On an individual level this means that long-term **regular smokers** can expect to **lose**, on average, **ten years of life**. About half to two-thirds of all long-term smokers die prematurely because of their smoking,

Table 2.1 Deaths attributable to smoking as a percentage of all deaths from that disease: England (1998–2002).

Cause of death	Percentages of deaths attributable to smoking	
	Men	Women
Cancers		
Lung	90	80
Throat and mouth	77	58
Oesophagus	70	72
Bladder	49	23
Kidney	42	7
Stomach	35	12
Pancreas	26	31
Leukaemia	19	12
Cardiovascular disease		
Ischaemic heart disease	21	12
Aortic aneurysm	64	65
Myocardial degeneration	26	18
Atherosclerosis	22	17
Stroke	10	8
Lung disease		
Bronchitis and emphysema	87	84
Pneumonia	26	17

Adapted from Twigg et al., 2004.

and do so on average 20 years earlier than if they did not smoke (Doll et al., 2004).

The **main causes of death** attributable to cigarette smoking are **cancers, cardiovascular disease** and **lung disease** (Table 2.1 and Figure 2.1).

The following sections discuss these, and some of the less common, causes of smoking-related death.

Figure 2.1 Proportion of UK deaths attributable to smoking by disease.

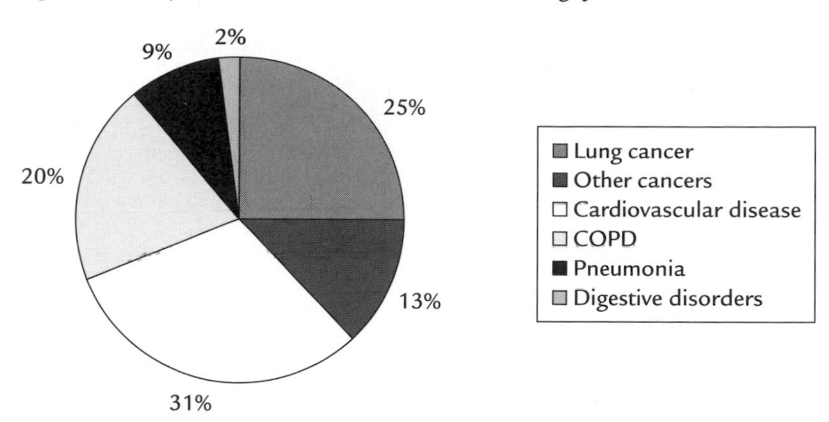

Royal College of Physicians, 2000.

2.1.1 Lung cancer

Lung cancer was almost unheard of before the smoking of manufactured cigarettes became popular at the beginning of the twentieth century. In the UK, in 2002, **lung cancer** caused about 34 000 deaths (Cancer Research UK, 2004): of these it can be estimated that **28 000 were caused by smoking**. The **risk** of contracting lung cancer **for a cigarette smoker** is **15 times greater** than that of a **non-smoker** (Boffetta et al., 1999). The risk accumulates over time and is related to both daily cigarette consumption (Sastre et al., 1999) and duration of smoking (Boffetta et al., 1999).

2.1.2 Cardiovascular disease

Cardiovascular disease is the **leading cause of death** in the UK, and accounts for nearly one-third of all smoking-related deaths. Cardiovascular diseases caused by smoking are listed in Table 2.2.

The average **smoker** has approximately **double the risk** of developing **heart disease** compared to someone who has never smoked (Wald & Hackshaw, 1996). The risk of developing a cardiovascular disease occurs even with very light smoking (Dunn et al., 1999), unlike lung cancer where the risk is directly proportional to overall smoke exposure.

Table 2.2 Estimated number and percentage of deaths attributable to smoking by cardiovascular disease, UK.

Cardiovascular disease	Number	As percentage of all deaths from disease		
		Men	Women	Total
Ischaemic heart disease	24 300	22	12	17
Cerebrovascular disease (stroke)	6 900	12	9	10
Aortic aneurysm	5 800	61	52	57
Myocardial degeneration	500	22	12	15
Atherosclerosis	200	15	7	10

Royal College of Physicians, 2000.

2.1.3 Chronic obstructive pulmonary disease (COPD)

COPD is smoking related for the most part, includes both chronic bronchitis and emphysema, and is a result of changes in central airways, peripheral airways, alveoli, capillaries and the immune system (USDHHS, 1990). In the UK in 2000, there were 24 300 deaths from **COPD** as a consequence of smoking, accounting for **over one-fifth of all smoking-related deaths** (Peto et al., 2004). Eighty-six percent of all deaths from COPD for men and 80% in women were smoking related (Royal College of Physicians, 2000). Smokers often talk of having a '**smoker's cough**'; this is usually a **sign of COPD** and they should have their **lung function tested** to see how much damage has already been done. If they wait until they are breathless they will already be well on the way to permanent disability.

I can see how smoking might be bad for your lungs, but how can it harm your heart?

Unfortunately it is not just the direct effect of tobacco smoke that causes the damage. There are some 4000 different chemicals in tobacco smoke that are absorbed into your bloodstream and find their way to all parts of the body where they cause damage. The effects of smoking can be seen in blood vessels, your heart and even your stomach. In women, components of tobacco smoke can also be found on the cervix.

2.1.4 Other life-threatening diseases

Carcinogens in cigarette smoke are ingested, dispersed and eliminated throughout the body, and therefore **smoking** is linked with a

Table 2.3 Estimated number and percentage of deaths attributable to smoking by cancer, UK 1997.

Cancer	Number	As percentage of all deaths from particular cancer		
		Men	Women	Total
Upper respiratory	1900	74	50	66
Oesophagus	4600	71	65	68
Bladder	1900	47	19	37
Kidney	800	40	6	27
Stomach	1900	35	11	26
Pancreas	1500	20	26	23
Unspecified site	3000	33	7	20
Myeloid leukaemia	300	19	11	15

Royal College of Physicians, 2000.

large number of cancers other than lung cancer (Table 2.3). Smoking is also a cause of non-cancerous but still life-threatening illnesses, such as ulcers of the stomach and duodenum (Chao et al., 2002).

I've got a relative who has smoked all their life and they are a ripe old age now. Anyway, we all have to die sometime don't we?

Most smokers know of a smoker who has lived into their eighties, but they tend to forget the many more smokers who have died before this – very old smokers are the exception. Even if dying early isn't a deterrent then it is worth remembering that smokers are unlikely to get the 'short but happy life' they are looking for – smokers' lives are not only shorter, but are unhealthier than non-smokers. So it is a 'short and unhappy life,' I am afraid.

2.2 Smoking morbidity

Approximately one-third of **lifelong smokers** avoid premature death despite their cigarette smoking (Peto et al., 2004), but **none escape** the **ill-health effects of smoking**. Smoking causes long-term disability, both in those smokers who are killed by smoking cigarettes and those who ultimately die from some other cause.

2.2.1 Non-life-threatening physical diseases linked to smoking

Lifelong chronic **smokers** can expect to **experience** diseases of **old age earlier than non-smokers**. Smoking impairs lung function, the circulatory system and the immune system. Smoking is strongly linked with non-fatal debilitating diseases including age-related deafness and blindness; smoking also causes wrinkles and makes smokers look older (Jorgensen et al., 1998). Box 2.1 lists non-fatal physical diseases linked to smoking.

Box 2.1 Non-life-threatening physical diseases linked to smoking.

- Age-related hearing loss
- Chronic back and neck pain
- Cataracts
- Cold injuries (tissue damage caused by exposure to cold environment)
- Crohn's disease (inflammatory bowel disease)
- Diabetes (type 2, non-insulin dependent)
- Erectile dysfunction
- Gum disease
- Macular degeneration (causing blindness)
- Osteoarthritis
- Osteoporosis
- Rheumatoid arthritis
- Skin wrinkling

ACSH, 1997.

In addition, smokers are at an increased risk of anaesthetic management problems during surgery (Rodrigo, 2000). Postoperatively, smoking patients' wounds heal more slowly (Silverstein, 1992) and they are more vulnerable to post-surgical complications than non-smokers (Moller et al., 2002).

2.2.2 Smoking and mental health

A large number of people with mental health problems smoke cigarettes (Figure 2.2). There exists a **strong link between smoking** and a range of psychiatric disorders, notably **mood disorders**,

Figure 2.2 Smoking prevalence in adults in the general population in the UK with a range of mental disorders.

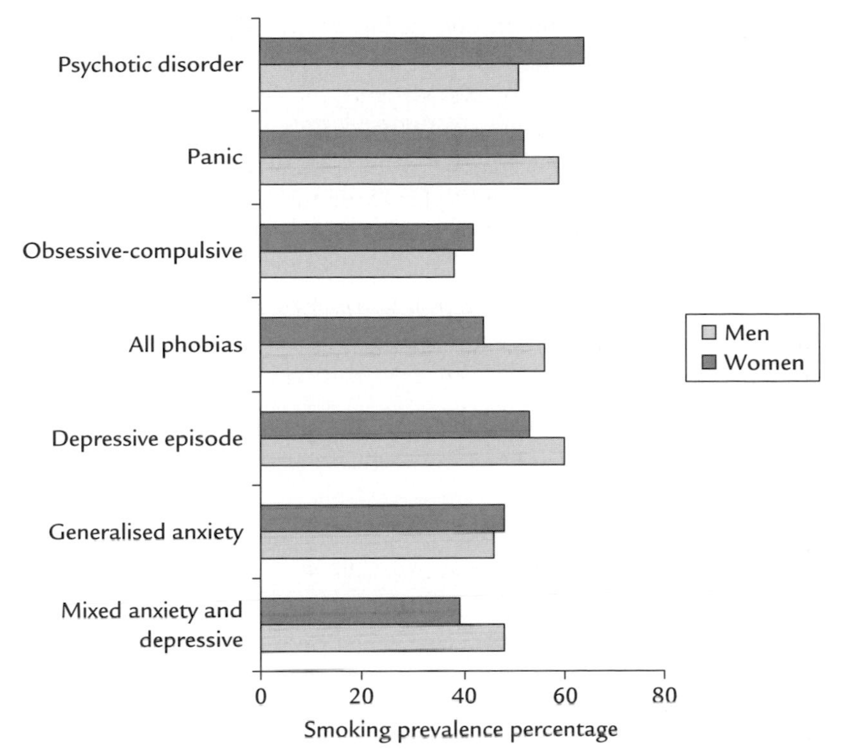

Meltzer, 1995.

schizophrenia and **alcohol and drug dependence**, but the nature of the relationship remains unclear. Whether smoking causes or exacerbates these conditions, whether they make it more likely that a sufferer will smoke, or whether there is a common underlying cause has yet to be established (West & Jarvis, in press). Low mood is also a withdrawal symptom and cases of major depression have been reported following smoking cessation (Glassman, 1993).

It is a widely held belief amongst smokers and non-smokers that smoking helps to relieve stress and anxiety (Pomerleau & Pomerleau, 1990). However, evidence suggests that **smoking does not help to reduce stress** (West, 1993); and that when **smokers** do **stop**, their **stress** and **anxiety** levels actually **decrease** (West & Hajek, 1997).

2.2.3 Reproductive health

Cigarette **smoking decreases the chances of conception** in both men and women. In male smokers it is linked to reduced sperm count

(Chia et al., 2000), and in women it is associated with hormonal effects that make pregnancy less likely (Barbieri, 2001). **Women who smoke** are **three times more likely** to take **over a year to conceive** than non-smokers (Baird & Wilcox, 1985).

It is widely recognised that cigarette smoking during pregnancy harms the fetus as well as the mother. The **health risks** posed by **smoking during pregnancy** are three-fold: to the **mother**, the **unborn child** and eventually the **newly born child** (Box 2.2).

Box 2.2 Ill-health effects of smoking prior to, during and after birth.

- Miscarriage
- Placental abruption (separation of placenta from uterus)
- Spontaneous abortion
- Ectopic pregnancy
- Placenta praevia (situated in the lower uterus and blocking uterine orifice)
- Premature rupture of the membranes
- Unexplained intra-uterine death
- Low birth-weight
- Unborn babies small for gestational age (resulting in problems of hypothermia and hypoglycaemia)
- Sudden infant death syndrome (cot death)
- Respiratory problems in infants
- Cardiovascular disease risk in adulthood
- Behavioural problems
- Impaired intellectual development

See Benowitz & Dempsey, 2004.

2.2.4 Environmental tobacco smoke

Exposure to cigarette smoke is not uncommon among non-smokers and they are at risk at home, at work, when socialising and in public places. **Parental smoking** is linked to increased risk of childhood **respiratory diseases** (Cook & Strachan, 1997) and **ear infections** (Department of Health, 1998). **Partner** and **occupational exposure** to tobacco smoke increases risk of **respiratory illness, lung cancer** and **coronary heart disease** (Department of Health, 1998). It is estimated that over 11 000 people die each year in the UK as a result of 'passive smoking' at home and at work (Jamrozik, 2005).

2.3 Health benefits of smoking cessation

Stopping smoking is the single **most important** thing a person can do to **improve** their **current and future health** (USDHHS, 1990). The greatest benefit is achieved in smokers with no smoking-related disease who stop smoking before they reach 35 years of age: they can have a normal life expectancy (Royal College of Physicians, 2000; Doll et al., 2004). However, smokers who stop later on in life than this, even into their seventies, can expect to significantly improve their life expectancy (USDHHS, 1990; Doll et al., 2004). (See Table 2.4.)

I have been smoking for over 20 years, there is no real point in stopping now is there as all the damage is done?

Your smoking may have done you some permanent damage, although this is no reason to continue smoking and do yourself further harm. Stopping smoking at whatever age will improve your health and increase your life expectancy.

Table 2.4 Beneficial health changes when you stop smoking.

Time since quitting	Beneficial health changes that take place
24 hours	Lungs start to clear out mucus and other smoking debris.
48 hours	Carbon monoxide will be eliminated from the body. Ability to taste and smell is greatly improved.
72 hours	Breathing becomes easier. Bronchial tubes begin to relax and energy levels increase.
2–12 weeks	Circulation improves.
3–9 months	Coughs, wheezing and breathing problems improve as lung function is increased by up to 10%.
1 year	Risk of a heart attack falls to about half that of a smoker.
10 years	Risk of lung cancer falls to half that of a smoker.
15 years	Risk of heart attack falls to the same as someone who has never smoked.

Adapted from Action on Smoking and Health (ASH) fact sheet.

2.3.1 Lung cancer

Compared with current smokers, **former smokers** show a significant **reduction in risk** of developing **lung cancer** (USDHHS, 1990). The greater the length of time having quit, the greater the reduction in risk of developing lung cancer; although this is also affected by the length of time a person had been smoking prior to stopping (Brown & Chu, 1987). A larger risk reduction is experienced by those who, when they smoked, inhaled less frequently and deeper, and who smoked fewer cigarettes (Lubin, 1984).

2.3.2 Cardiovascular disease

Ex-smokers have a **reduced risk** of **coronary heart disease** compared with current smokers (Cook et al., 1986). The risk of dying from cardiovascular disease decreases as the number of years since cessation of smoking increases (Paganini-Hill & Hsu, 1994), but even **within 12 months of stopping** smoking the **risk of sudden death** from a cardiac event is **reduced** (USDHHS, 1990). The risk of cerebrovascular disease (stroke) is significantly lower among former smokers compared with current smokers (Wolfe et al., 1988).

So if I stop smoking, will my blood pressure go down?

You may not see any changes in your blood pressure, at least not immediately. However, blood pressure does rise temporarily after each cigarette, and so with stopping smoking you will be putting less strain on your heart. The longer you go without smoking the better your heart and blood vessels will be. Your risk of having a heart attack or stroke will decline over time, and your cardiovascular system will have an improved performance.

2.3.3 Chronic obstructive pulmonary disease (COPD)

Stopping smoking significantly reduces the risk of dying from COPD compared with continuing smoking, but does not reduce it to the level of those who have never smoked, even after twenty years or more of abstinence (USDHHS, 1990). For sufferers of COPD **stopping smoking** has the almost immediate effect of **preventing continued steep decline in lung function** (USDHHS, 1990) and **reducing** respiratory symptoms, such as **cough** and **shortness of breath** (Anthonisen et al., 1994).

2.3.4 Other life-threatening diseases

The **reduction** in the **risk** of dying associated with **stopping smoking** is not confined to the three main causes of death; it extends to **other cancers** as well. Smoking cessation results in a significant reduction, compared with continuing smoking, in the risk of death from cancers of the upper respiratory tract, oesophagus, bladder and pancreas. A smaller, but still significant, reduction in risk is also reported for multiple primary cancers, myeloid leukaemia, kidney cancer and bladder cancer (USDHHS, 1990). In addition, the mortality risk for peptic ulcers is 50% lower among former smokers than current smokers (USDHHS, 1988); the benefits of stopping smoking on the risk of death from duodenal ulcers is also well established (USDHHS, 1990). Smoking cessation has also been shown to result in regression of low-grade cervical abnormalities (pre-cancerous lesions) (Szarewski et al., 1996).

2.3.5 Smoking cessation and reproductive health

Stopping smoking before the thirtieth week of gestation **increases birth-weight** of newborn babies when compared with babies of continuing smokers, and **decreases the chances** of **preterm delivery** (MacArthur & Knox, 1988) and **sudden infant death syndrome** (SIDS) (DiFranza & Lew, 1995). Ex-smokers are also less likely to experience complications of childbirth, such as placenta praevia and abruption, than those pregnant women who continue to smoke (Naeye, 1980).

2.3.6 Smoking cessation and mental health

There is some evidence that individuals with a history of depression who stop smoking experience a worsening of depressive symptoms; however, other research has found that episodes of depression are no more common after quitting than while still smoking (Tsoh et al., 2000). There is clear evidence that **ex-smokers** are **mentally healthier** than current smokers (USDHHS, 1990).

2.3.7 Morbidity and smoking cessation

Stopping smoking doesn't just add *years* to *life*, it adds *life* to *years*. Ex-smokers can not only expect a longer life than those who continue to smoke, but a healthier one as well (USDHHS, 1990). **Former smokers** experience **fewer days of illness** (USDHHS, 1988) and are **absent from work less** (Gallop, 1989) than current smokers.

2.3.8 The protective effects of smoking

There is a negative association between cigarette smoking and the risk of Parkinson's disease (Hernan et al., 2001), most likely because of the dopaminergic action of nicotine (Maggio et al., 1998). Cigarette smoking also appears to have a protective effect against ulcerative colitis (Calkins, 1989), possibly due to changes in bowel mucus or prostaglandins and immune suppression (Rhodes, 1997). Furthermore, rates of pre-eclampsia are higher in non-smokers than in smokers; however, smokers with pre-eclampsia suffer higher rates of placental abruption and have higher rates of very low birth-weight babies (Newman et al., 2001). Indeed, the health **risks** of continued **smoking** far **outweigh** all of these **apparently protective effects** (USDHHS, 1990).

2.4 Sources for updating health information and statistics

- Cancer — Cancer Research UK (www.cancerresearchuk.org)
- Coronary heart disease — British Heart Foundation (www.bhf.org.uk)
- General information — Action on Smoking and Health (ASH) (www.ash.org.uk)

The Health Consequences of Smoking: A Report of the Surgeon General (27 May, 2004). United States Department of Health & Human Services (www.surgeongeneral.gov/library/smokingconsequences)

2.5 Multiple choice questions

Question 1: In the UK smoking is responsible for how many deaths per year?

a 126 000

b 120 000

c 106 000

d 100 000

e 96 000

Question 2: How many years of life, on average, can more than half of all long-term smokers be expected to lose as a result of their smoking?

a 3 years

b 5 years

c 6 years

d 10 years

e 20 years

Question 3: Regarding lung cancer, which of the following statements is TRUE?

a Lung cancer was a common cause of death before cigarettes were introduced

b 25% of all lung cancers are related to smoking

c The risk of lung cancer in a smoker is five times that of a non-smoker

d The risk of lung cancer is related to cigarette consumption and number of years of smoking

e The risk of lung cancer is primarily related to the type of cigarette smoked

Question 4: Regarding cardiovascular disease, which of the following statements is TRUE?

a Cardiovascular disease primarily affects those who smoke more than 20 cigarettes per day

b For a smoker the risk of developing cardiovascular disease is 15 times greater than a non-smoker

c Cardiovascular disease is the second major cause of death in the UK after cancer

d Nicotine has not been proven to cause cardiovascular disease

e Among smokers, women are at higher risk of developing cardiovascular disease than men

Question 5: Smoking is associated with an increased risk of all but which one of the following diseases?

a Erectile dysfunction

b Ulcerative colitis

c Crohn's disease

d Rheumatoid arthritis

e Skin wrinkling

Question 6: Which of the following cancers is not known to be caused by smoking?

- **a** Testicular cancer
- **b** Bladder cancer
- **c** Oesophageal cancer
- **d** Lung cancer
- **e** Stomach cancer

Question 7: Regarding smoking and mental health, which of the following statements is FALSE?

- **a** Smokers are more likely to have a diagnosis of depression than non-smokers
- **b** People with depression are more likely to smoke than those without mental health problems
- **c** Stopping smoking can result in depression
- **d** Stopping smoking causes an increase in anxiety
- **e** Smoking prevalence is high in those with psychiatric disorders

Question 8: Regarding smoking and reproductive health, which of the following statements is FALSE?

- **a** Smoking is associated with an increased risk of pre-eclampsia in pregnancy
- **b** Smoking is linked to a reduced sperm count in men
- **c** Smoking during pregnancy is associated with an increased risk of low birth-weight babies
- **d** Smoking during pregnancy is linked with behavioural problems in the infant
- **e** Smoking during pregnancy is associated with premature rupture of the membranes

Question 9: Regarding environmental tobacco smoke, which of the following statements is FALSE?

- **a** It is associated with an increased risk of childhood respiratory disease
- **b** It is associated with an increased risk of lung cancer
- **c** Each year an estimated 11 000 people die as a result of second-hand smoke exposure
- **d** Smoking in only one room of the house removes the risk to children of environmental tobacco smoke
- **e** It is associated with an increased risk of ear infections in the children of smokers

Question 10: Stopping smoking is associated with all but which one of the following?

- **a** A 50% reduced risk of having a heart attack within a year of stopping
- **b** A 50% reduced risk of lung cancer within a year of stopping

c Improvement in circulation

d Improvement in breathing

e Decreased rate of decline in lung function

Question 11: Regarding life-threatening diseases and stopping smoking, which of the following statements is FALSE?

a There is a greater reduction in risk of oesophageal cancer than kidney cancer

b There is a 50% reduction of mortality risk associated with peptic ulcer disease

c There is no reduction in the risk of myeloid leukaemia

d Stopping smoking can reverse early pre-cancerous lesions of the cervix

e There is a reduction in the risk of death from duodenal ulcers

Question 12: Which of the following statements is FALSE?

a In order to reduce the risk of low birth-weight babies, it is best if pregnant smokers stop in the first trimester

b Stopping smoking reduces the risk of cot death

c Ex-smokers are mentally healthier than current smokers

d Ex-smokers are absent from work less than current smokers

e Smoking is associated with a reduced risk of developing Parkinson's disease

References

ACSH (1997). *Cigarettes: What the Warning Label Doesn't Tell You*. New York: American Council on Science & Health.

Anthonisen, N.R., Connett, J.E., Kiley, J.P., Altose, M.D., Bailey, W.C., Buist, A.S., et al. (1994). Effects of smoking intervention and the use of an inhaled anticholinergic bronchodilator on the rate of decline of FEV1. The Lung Health Study. *Journal of American Medical Association, 16 Nov. 272* (19):1497–1505.

Baird, D.D. & Wilcox, A.J. (1985). Cigarette smoking associated with delayed conception. *Journal of American Medical Association, 253* (20), 2979–2983.

Barbieri, R.L. (2001). The initial fertility consultation: recommendations concerning cigarette smoking, body mass index, and alcohol and caffeine consumption. *American Journal of Obstetric Gynecology, 185* (5), 1168–1173.

Benowitz, N. & Dempsey, D. (2004). Pharmacotherapy for smoking cessation during pregnancy. *Nicotine & Tobacco Research, April, 6* (Suppl. 2), S189–202.

Boffetta, P., Pershagen, G., Jockel, K.H., Forastiere, F., Gaborieau, V., Heinrich, J., et al. (1999). Cigar and pipe smoking and lung cancer

risk: a multi-centre study from Europe. *Journal of National Cancer Institute*, *91* (8), 697–701.
Brown, C. & Chu, K. (1987). Use of multi-stage models to infer stage affected by carcinogenic exposure: example of lung cancer and cigarette smoking. *Journal of Chronic Disease*, *40* (Suppl. 2), S171–179.
Calkins, B.M. (1989). A meta-analysis of the role of smoking in inflammatory bowel disease. *Digestive Diseases Science, Dec.*, *34* (12), 1841–1854.
Cancer Research UK (2004). *CancerStats: Mortality – UK*. London: Cancer Research UK.
Chao, A., Thun, M.J., Henley, S.J., Jacobs, E.J., McCullough, M.L. & Calle, E.E. (2002). Cigarette smoking, use of other tobacco products and stomach cancer mortality in US adults: The Cancer Prevention Study II. *International Journal of Cancer*, *101* (4), 380–389.
Chia, S.E., Lim, S.T. & Tay, S.K. (2000). Factors associated with male infertility: a case-control study of 218 infertile and 240 fertile men. *Bjog*, *107* (1), 55–61.
Cook, D.G., Shaper, A.G., Pocock, S.J. & Kussick, S.J. (1986). Giving up smoking and the risk of heart attacks. A report from the British Regional Heart Study. *Lancet*, *13* (2 (8520)), 1376–1380.
Cook, D.G. & Strachan, D.P. (1997). Health effects of passive smoking. 3. Parental smoking and prevalence of respiratory symptoms and asthma in schoolage children. *Thorax*, *52* (12), 1081–1094.
Department of Health (1998). *Smoking Kills: A White Paper on Tobacco*. London: The Stationery Office.
DiFranza, J.R. & Lew, R.A. (1995). Effect of maternal cigarette smoking on pregnancy complications and sudden infant death syndrome. *The Journal of Family Practice*, *40* (4), 385–394.
Doll, R., Peto, R., Boreham, J. & Sutherland, I. (2004). Mortality in relation to smoking: 50 years' observations on male British doctors. *British Medical Journal*, *328* (7455), 1519.
Dunn, N., Thorogood, M., Faragher, B., de Caestecker, L., MacDonald, T.M., McCollum, C., et al. (1999). Oral contraceptives and myocardial infarction: results of the MICA case-control study. *British Medical Journal*, *318* (7198), 1579–1583.
Gallop, B. (1989). Sickness absenteeism and smoking. *New Zealand Medical Journal*, *102* (863), 112.
Glassman, A.H. (1993). Cigarette smoking: implications for psychiatric illness. *American Journal of Psychiatry*, *150* (4), 546–553.
Hernan, M.A., Zhang, S.M., Rueda-deCastro, A.M., Colditz, G.A., Speizer, F.E. & Ascherio, A. (2001). Cigarette smoking and the incidence of Parkinson's disease in two prospective studies. *Annals of Neurology*, *50* (6), 780–786.
Jamrozik, K. (2005). Estimate of deaths attributable to passive smoking among UK adults: database analysis. *British Medical Journal*, doi:10.1136/bmj.38370.496632.8F (published 2 March 2005).
Jorgensen, L.N., Kallehave, F., Christensen, E., Siana, J.E. & Gottrup, F. (1998). Less collagen production in smokers. *Surgery, April*, *123* (4), 450–455.

Lubin, J. (1984). Modifying risk of developing lung cancer by changing habits of cigarette smoking. *British Medical Journal (Clinical Research Edition)*, *289* (6449), 921.

MacArthur, C. & Knox, E.G. (1988). Effects of stopping at different stages. *British Journal of Obstetrics and Gynaecology*, *95* (6), 551–555.

Maggio, R., Riva, M., Vaglini, F., Fornai, F., Molteni, R., Armogida, M., et al. (1998). Nicotine prevents experimental Parkinsonism in rodents and induces striatal increase of neurotrophic factors. *Journal of Neurochemistry*, *71* (6), 2439–2446.

Meltzer, H. (1995). *OPCS Surveys of Psychiatric Morbidity in Great Britain Report 1: The Prevalence of Psychiatric Morbidity Among Adults Living in Private Households*. London: HMSO.

Moller, A.M., Villebro, N., Pedersen, T. & Tonnesen, H. (2002). Effect of pre-operative smoking intervention on post-operative complications: a randomised clinical trial. *Lancet*, *359* (9301), 114–117.

Naeye, R.L. (1980). Abruptio placentae and placenta previa: frequency, perinatal mortality, and cigarette smoking. *Obstetrics and Gynecology*, *55* (6), 701–704.

Newman, M.G., Lindsay, M.K. & Graves, W. (2001). Cigarette smoking and pre-eclampsia: their association and effects on clinical outcomes. *Journal of Maternal and Fetal Medicine*, *10* (3), 166–170.

Paganini-Hill, A. & Hsu, G. (1994). Smoking and mortality among residents of a California retirement community. *American Journal of Public Health*, *84* (6), 992–995.

Peto, R., Lopez, A., Boreham, J. & Thun, M. (2004). *Mortality from Smoking in Developed Countries 1950–2000* (2nd edn). Oxford: Oxford University Press.

Pomerleau, O.F. & Pomerleau, C.S. (1990). Behavioural studies in humans: anxiety, stress and smoking. *Ciba Foundation Symposium*, *152*, 225–235; discussion 235–229.

Rhodes, J.M. (1997). Colonic mucus and ulcerative colitis. *Gut*, *40* (6), 807–808.

Rodrigo, C. (2000). The effects of cigarette smoking on anesthesia. *Anesthesia Progress*, *Winter*, *47* (4), 143–150.

Royal College of Physicians (2000). *Nicotine Addiction in Britain*. London: Royal College of Physicians.

Sastre, M., Mullet, E. & Sorum, P. (1999). Relationship between cigarette dose and perceived risk of lung cancer. *Preventive Medicine*, *28* (6), 566–571.

Silverstein, P. (1992). Smoking and wound healing. *American Journal of Medicine*, *15 July*, *93* (1A), S22–24.

Szarewski, A., Jarvis, M.J. & Sasieni, P. et al. (1996). Effect of smoking cessation on cervical lesion size, *Lancet*. *347*, 941–943.

Tsoh, J.Y., Humfleet, G.L., Munoz, R.F., Reus, V.I., Hartz, D. T. & Hall, S.M. (2000). Development of major depression after treatment for smoking cessation. *American Journal of Psychiatry*, *157* (3), 368–374.

Twigg, L., Moon, G. & Walker, S. (2004). The smoking epidemic in England. London: Health Development Agency.

USDHHS (1988). *The Health Consequence of Smoking: Nicotine Addiction. A Report of the Surgeon General*. Rockville, Md.: US Department of Health and Human Services.

USDHHS (1990). *The Health Benefits of Smoking Cessation: A Report of the Surgeon General*. Rockville, Md.: US Department of Health and Human Services.

USDHHS (2004). *The Health Consequences of Smoking: A Report of the Surgeon General*. Atlanta, Ga.: US Department of Health and Human Services, Centres for Disease Control and Prevention, National Centre for Chronic Disease Prevention and Health Promotion, Office on Smoking and Health.

Wald, N. & Hackshaw, A. (1996). Cigarette smoking: an epidemiological overview. In: Doll, R. (Ed.), *Tobacco and Health*, *52* (1), 3–11. London: British Medical Bulletin.

West, R. (1993). Beneficial effects of nicotine: fact or fiction? *Addiction*, *88* (5), 589–590.

West, R. & Hajek, P. (1997). What happens to anxiety levels on giving up smoking? *American Journal of Psychiatry*, *154* (11), 1589–1592.

West, R. & Jarvis, M. (in press). Tobacco smoking and mental disorder. *The Italian Journal of Psychiatry and Behavioural Sciences*.

Wolfe, P., D'Agostino, R., Kannel, W., Bonita, R. & Belanger, W. (1988). Cigarette smoking as a risk factor for stroke: the Framingham study. *Journal of American Medical Association*, *259* (7), 1025–1029.

Part Two:
Practical Advice

Chapter 3

Brief interventions

This chapter provides information necessary for health professionals to carry out brief opportunistic interventions with smokers. It also draws on good clinical practice to suggest what the content of such brief interventions may be. Smoking cessation guidelines recommend that **all health professionals** should **check on the smoking status** of their clients **at least once a year** and **advise smokers to stop** (West et al., 2000). This **brief advice** from a health professional should be **delivered opportunistically** during routine consultations to smokers **whether or not** they are **seeking help with stopping smoking**.

Evidence only exists for the effectiveness of brief smoking cessation advice from GPs. **Brief advice** (up to five minutes) **from a GP** leads between **1%** and **3%** of patients receiving it to **stop smoking** for at least six months (Silagy, 2000). **This advice appears to have its effect primarily by triggering a quit attempt** rather than by increasing the chances of success of quit attempts. The key elements of brief smoking cessation advice are:

(1) **Ask** if the person smokes

(2) **Advise** smokers to quit

(3) If they would like help **refer** them to the NHS Stop Smoking Service, or if they do not want to attend the service, then **where possible** offer an alternative

See Figure 3.1 for information on brief advice.

3.1 Assessment and recording of smoking status

The **assessment** and **recording** of **smoking status** is important in its own right, but it also provides an **opportunity to intervene with smokers**.

Figure 3.1 Brief advice flow chart.

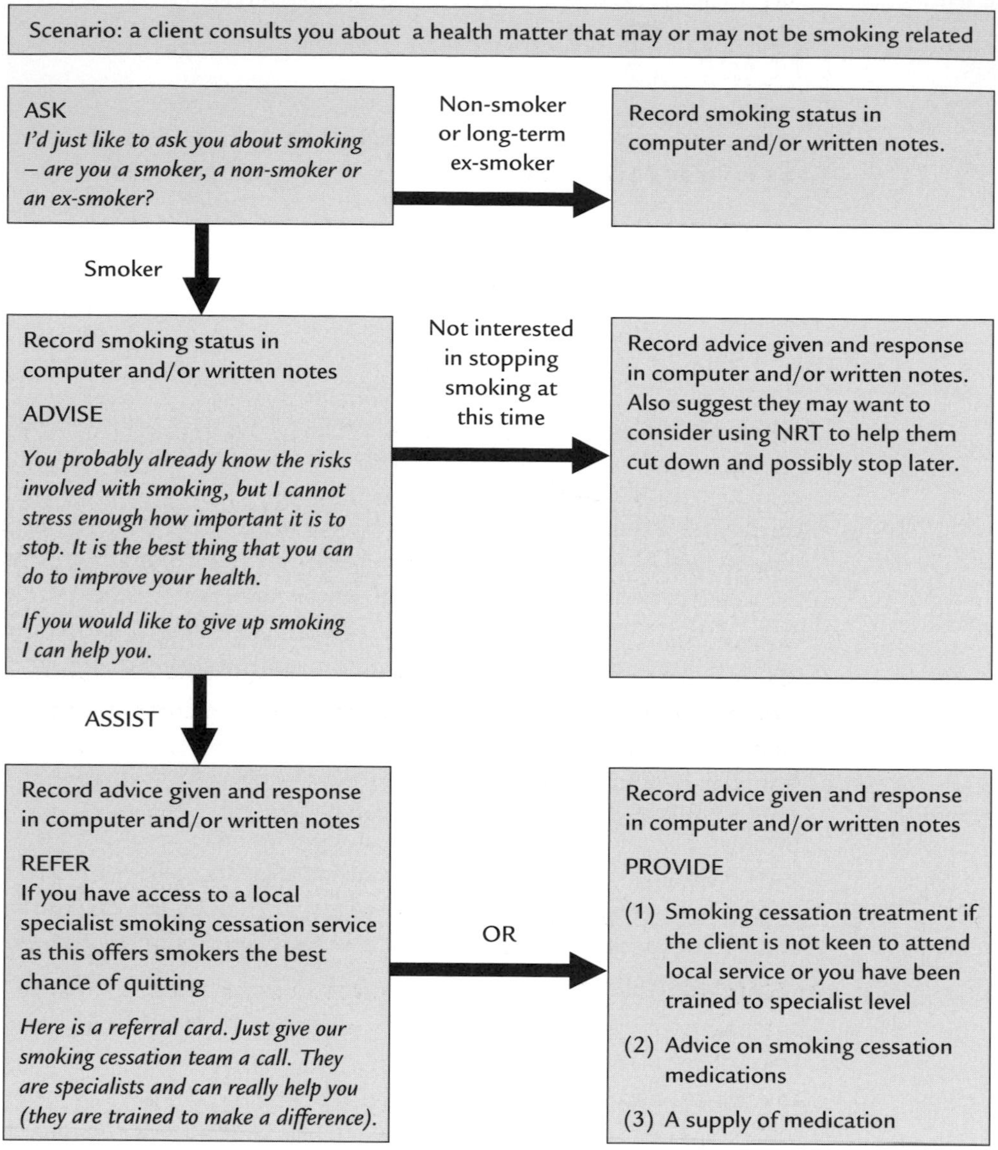

Scenario: a client consults you about a health matter that may or may not be smoking related

ASK
I'd just like to ask you about smoking – are you a smoker, a non-smoker or an ex-smoker?

Non-smoker or long-term ex-smoker →

Record smoking status in computer and/or written notes.

Smoker ↓

Record smoking status in computer and/or written notes

ADVISE

You probably already know the risks involved with smoking, but I cannot stress enough how important it is to stop. It is the best thing that you can do to improve your health.

If you would like to give up smoking I can help you.

Not interested in stopping smoking at this time →

Record advice given and response in computer and/or written notes. Also suggest they may want to consider using NRT to help them cut down and possibly stop later.

ASSIST ↓

Record advice given and response in computer and/or written notes

REFER
If you have access to a local specialist smoking cessation service as this offers smokers the best chance of quitting

Here is a referral card. Just give our smoking cessation team a call. They are specialists and can really help you (they are trained to make a difference).

OR →

Record advice given and response in computer and/or written notes

PROVIDE

(1) Smoking cessation treatment if the client is not keen to attend local service or you have been trained to specialist level

(2) Advice on smoking cessation medications

(3) A supply of medication

3.1.1 Asking about smoking status

Health professionals should **ask about smoking** in an **appropriate way**, to elicit an **accurate response**. The way this is done is going to differ slightly depending on who is asking the question and in what situation; health professionals should use their existing clinical skills to carry out this assessment. The following statement box gives an example of asking about smoking status for a **first contact with client**.

Do you smoke cigarettes or tobacco at all, or have you ever smoked regularly?

The statement box below gives an example of asking about smoking status for an **existing client**.

Are you still smoking/not smoking?

There are objective markers of smoking status, such as expired air carbon monoxide tests (see Section 4.2.4) and urine or saliva tests that measure cotinine (a metabolite of nicotine). There are also observations that health professionals can make: namely the smell of cigarettes on clients' clothes and hair. Additionally, for dental health staff, for example, leucoplakia, smoker's palate and teeth staining.

Smoking status of clients should be **checked** as frequently as the health professional deems **appropriate**, but **at least every 12 months.** A more frequent assessment of smoking status is recommended for clients with common smoking-related conditions: coronary heart disease, stroke and transient cerebral ischaemic attack, hypertension, diabetes mellitus and chronic obstructive pulmonary disease.

3.1.2 Recording smoking status

Clients' smoking status should be recorded in written and/or computer notes as a **smoker**, long-term **ex-smoker** (>12 months), **recent ex-smoker** (12 months or less), or **non-smoker**. **Smokers** should be **advised to stop smoking** (see Section 3.2 below). **Congratulate ex-smokers**; positive reinforcement is usually welcome. For **ex-smokers** and **non-smokers** a record of the date on which their **smoking status** was established **should be noted**; this will allow for a comparison when **questioned** in the future (**at least every 12 months**). In the statement box below is an example of a response to a client who reports being a **non-smoker**.

Well done for not smoking. As you probably know smoking is one of the most harmful things that you can do.

An example of a response to a client who reports being an **ex-smoker** is shown in the statement box below.

Well done for not smoking. Staying an ex-smoker will mean a lot for your future health.

The preferred **Read codes** for smoking status are shown in Table 3.1.

Table 3.1 Read codes.

Never smoked	1371
Ex-smoker	137S
Smoker	137R

3.2 Advising smokers to stop and assessing interest in quitting

Smokers may be more **receptive to advice** to stop when it is **linked with an existing medical condition** (**not necessarily smoking related**) and are happier to receive advice to stop when GPs link the advice to their reason for visiting the surgery (Butler et al., 1998). There is some evidence, amongst GPs, that repeating the advice with a given smoker may have a reduced effect.

3.2.1 Advising clients to stop smoking

Any client identified as a **smoker** should be **advised to stop** smoking. What is said and the way it is said will depend upon the health professional giving the advice, the smoker receiving it and the situation in which it is given. Health professionals will use their experience and clinical skills when giving such advice, but a few examples are listed opposite. The statement box following gives examples of **advising a smoker to stop**.

You probably already know the risks involved with smoking, but I cannot stress enough how important it is to stop. It is the best thing that you can do to improve your health.

The best thing you can do for your health is to stop smoking, and I would advise you to stop as soon as possible.

Quitting smoking will substantially decrease the risk of you developing cancer, heart disease and lung disease. You could also save a lot of money – a 20-a-day smoker will save at least £1500 per year.

Most smokers want to give up smoking at some point. You might want to think about stopping smoking sooner rather than later.

As your doctor/nurse/pharmacist/name of health profession it is my duty to advise you to stop smoking. Stopping smoking is the single best thing that you can do to improve your current and future health. ”

Some **situations** in which **brief advice** to stop smoking **can be offered** are shown in Table 3.2.

Table 3.2 Opportunities for brief advice to stop smoking.

Health professional	Opportunities for brief smoking cessation advice
GP	Any routine consultation, consultations that are smoking related (e.g. breathlessness, chest infection etc.), when conducting regular (at least yearly) check of smoking status. Screening checks are also a good opportunity to raise the issue, such as having a cervical smear test (as smoking is linked to cervical cancer).
Practice nurse	Any routine consultation, attendance for cholesterol testing, consultations concerning the health of a smoking client's child, when conducting regular (at least yearly) check of smoking status.
Community pharmacist	Any routine consultation or interest shown in nicotine replacement therapy (NRT) products on display. Also, presentation of prescription for medicine treating smoking-related condition (e.g. GTN for angina) or non-smoking-related condition (e.g. oral contraceptive pill as there is an increased risk of deep vein thrombosis (DVT) in women who smoke).
Dentist	Any routine consultation, whilst cleaning teeth that are stained from smoking, when any consequence of smoking upon oral health (e.g. periodontal disease and leucoplakia) is observed, when conducting regular (at least yearly) check of smoking status.

3.2.2 Assessment of interest in quitting

Having advised a smoker to stop, the next task for the health professional is to enquire whether the client is interested in stopping smoking. The statement box below gives examples of **assessing interest in quitting**.

If you would like to give up smoking I can help you.

If you are interested in stopping smoking there are services and medications which can help you in your quit attempt. Would you be interested in stopping smoking?

Tobacco is very addictive, so it can be very difficult to give up, and many people have to try several times before they succeed. Your chances of succeeding are much greater if you make use of counselling support, which I can arrange for you, and either nicotine replacement therapy (NRT) or the drug bupropion (Zyban), which can be prescribed for you.

The NHS provides free and effective treatment for smokers like yourself. In fact you are up to four times more likely to quit using this help than quitting by yourself. Are you interested in such help?

In most cases clients' responses to advice to stop smoking will fall neatly into one of the following categories: **do not want to stop smoking, not interested in stopping smoking at this time** and **interested in stopping smoking**. Where the responses from clients to advice to stop are less clear, health professionals will need to use their clinical judgement to assess the clients' interest in stopping smoking. In such cases it may be worth noting that stop smoking advice was given, that the client appeared uncertain about what they wanted to do and that they should be asked again about stopping smoking at the next consultation.

Should I go ahead with my quit attempt even though I feel that this is not a good time for me to try to stop smoking?

If you do not feel that you are ready to stop smoking then you should wait. Stopping smoking takes a lot of determination and works best if you are 100% ready to quit. On the other hand there is never really a 'good time' to stop smoking and you should not continually postpone stopping smoking by waiting for the 'right time'.

When clients respond that they **do not want to stop smoking** or are **not interested in stopping smoking at this time** then they can be informed that **NRT** products are now available to **help smokers cut down** the amount of cigarettes that they smoke, with a view to **stopping smoking** completely in the **long term** (see Sections 3.3.2 and 3.5.2).

3.2.3 Recording advice given and responses

If a smoker replies that they are **not interested in stopping smoking**, or that they are **not interested** in stopping smoking **at this time**, then the advice given and the response received should be recorded in written and/or computer notes. These clients can then be **advised** once more to consider stopping smoking **in the future** (within 12 months).

If a client states that they **do want to stop smoking** then this should be **recorded** in their notes so that an **enquiry** can be made at the next meeting or consultation as to **how their quit attempt went.**

If a client expresses the wish to **cut down** the amount that they smoke **using NRT** before **stopping completely**, then this should also be recorded in their notes and an **enquiry** as to how they are progressing should be made at the **next consultation or meeting**.

The **Read code** for giving **smoking cessation advice is** 8CAL.

3.3 Compensatory smoking

3.3.1 Evidence of compensatory smoking

Because smokers are used to regular doses of nicotine they subconsciously ensure that they receive similar amounts of nicotine from the reduced number of cigarettes they are now smoking, so they also get similar amounts of tar and carbon monoxide. **Smokers compensate for the reduced number of cigarettes by smoking each cigarette more intensively** (Benowitz et al., 1986). Cigarettes can be smoked more intensively by drawing harder and longer on the cigarette, taking more puffs per cigarette, holding the smoke in the lungs longer and smoking the cigarette nearer to the filter.

3.3.2 Cutting down

A large majority of health professionals advise smokers to cut down if they think that their clients are unwilling or unable to stop completely (McEwen & West, 2001). **One-third** (33%) of **smokers** each year **try to reduce** the number of **cigarettes** they smoke (ONS, 2004). Unfortunately, **cutting down** the **number of cigarettes** smoked without providing nicotine in some other form is **unlikely to bring significant health benefits** and smokers almost invariably resume their previous level of consumption quickly (West & McEwen, 1999). However, it is apparent that if smokers manage to cut down with the help of NRT they are more likely to stop later.

Similarly, **many smokers believe** that switching to **lower-tar cigarettes** is a **healthier option**. But this is **not** the case – **compensatory smoking occurs** in this situation as well, with smokers smoking their cigarettes more efficiently, resulting in equivalent levels of health risk.

The **best advice** to give is to **stop smoking completely** and that there are **specialist services** that provide evidence-based treatment to help smokers achieve this goal. However, for those **smokers** who **do not** currently wish to **quit** they should be informed of the option of using **NRT to help them cut down**, with the goal of **stopping completely** in the long term (6–12 months). See Box 3.1. The statement box below gives an example of informing a smoker about **compensatory smoking**.

It may seem like a good idea to cut down the number of cigarettes that you smoke or to switch to 'lighter' (lower tar) cigarettes – but it is not that simple. Because your mind and body are used to regular doses of nicotine you will ensure that you continue to get similar amounts of nicotine from these fewer, or 'lighter', cigarettes by smoking them more intensely. ”

Box 3.1 An exception – cutting down, then stopping, using NRT.

Some NRT products are now licensed for helping smokers to cut down the amount of cigarettes they smoke with the aim of stopping completely in the long term (see **Section 4.3.1 NRT**). NRT can help smokers to 'truly' cut down because it provides them with an alternative source of nicotine that they therefore do not have to get from their cigarettes.

The option of using NRT to cut down and then stop should not be offered as a first line of treatment, but rather offered to those smoking clients who state that they are unwilling or unable to stop smoking.

3.4 Reasons why stopping smoking can be difficult

Smokers' own beliefs about the benefits of smoking, the nature of nicotine dependence and the withdrawal symptoms experienced when smokers stop, all combine to make stopping smoking an extremely difficult process for most smokers.

3.4.1 Perceived benefits of smoking

A large number of smokers attending an NHS Stop Smoking Clinic were asked to rate the importance of various motives to their smoking on a scale between 1 (not at all) and 5 (yes, very much) (see Figure 3.2). Enjoyment, boredom relief and stress relief were the highest, but **none of them predict relapse**. Enjoyment of smoking is not related to ability to maintain abstinence.

The special case of 'stress relief'

- Many smokers report that they smoke because it helps them cope with stress.

Figure 3.2 Self-reported smoking motives.

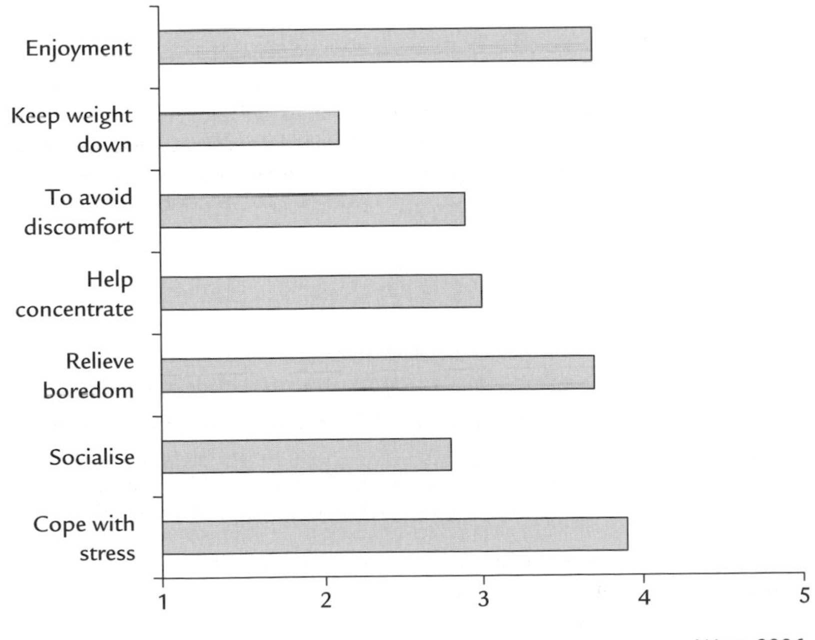

West, 2006.

- However, ex-smokers and non-smokers are less stressed than smokers.
- Smokers who maintain complete abstinence for four weeks report significant reduction in anxiety compared with before they stopped smoking.
- Smokers who continue to smoke at a low level report an increase in anxiety above pre-cessation levels.

The statement box below gives an example of what to say to a smoker about **stress relief**.

Most smokers say that one of the main reasons that they smoke is to help them cope with stress. However, we know that once people stop smoking they are less stressed than when they smoked.

3.4.2 Nicotine dependence

If cigarettes did not deliver nicotine, they would not be smoked and smokers would not find it so hard to stop. Nicotine is a drug that attacks the central and peripheral nervous system, mimicking, to some degree, a naturally occurring chemical messenger called acetylcholine (ACh).

Nerve cells communicate with each other by means of these chemical messengers – they are released from one cell and attach to a specially designed 'receptor' in the other cell, rather like a key fitting into a lock. Once they have attached to that receptor they can do a number of things, including causing the nerve cell hosting the receptor to become activated.

Of particular interest in the case of nicotine are cells whose cell bodies are in the midbrain region called the ventral tegmental area (VTA), whose fibres project forward to a region called the nucleus accumbens (NAcc) (see Figure 3.3).

I don't feel like an addict, smoking is just a habit isn't it?

Nicotine is an addictive drug and most regular smokers will be dependent upon it – whether they feel that way or not. Try going without a cigarette for a while; the levels of nicotine in your blood will drop, you will experience some withdrawal symptoms (especially the urge to smoke) and you might start to feel more like an 'addict'. Of course, having a cigarette will make these unpleasant withdrawal symptoms go away – which is what most smokers do in order to avoid feeling like this.

Figure 3.3 Representation of the mesolimbic dopamine pathway.

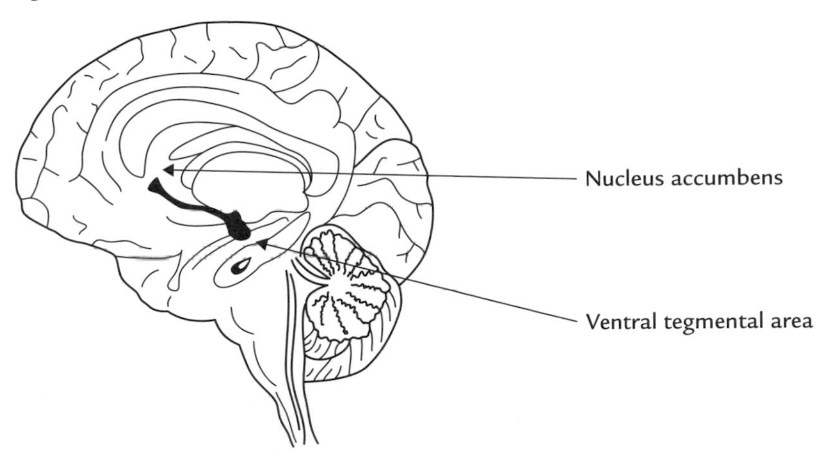

When smokers **puff on a cigarette** the **nicotine** is absorbed very quickly from the lungs into the bloodstream and **carried to the brain** within 20 seconds. It gets into the space between the nerve cells and attaches to the nicotinic-acetylcholine receptors in the VTA. This makes the nerve cells **release** another chemical messenger called **dopamine** at the other end in the NAcc, and this makes **cigarette smoking rewarding**.

Dopamine release in the NAcc has been found to have a profound effect on animal and human behaviour – it is a **signal** that tells the animal or the person to notice what caused it and to try and **repeat it**. In the case of smoking, that action is smoking a cigarette. All of this goes on at an **unconscious level. Nicotine rewards smoking, causing it to be repeated.** It is important to note that smokers do not need to feel pleasure for this effect to occur – it is an automatic process.

But this is just the start of the story. In many smokers the **nicotine alters the brain** so that smokers acquire a kind of '**drive**' to smoke, much like hunger. This means that if a smoker has not smoked for a while the drive increases, which makes the smoker want a cigarette and causes them to feel an **urge to smoke**. Like hunger, this drive can be kept at bay when smokers are distracted and it can be made worse when smokers are bored or reminded about cigarettes. The brains of smokers are also modified so that smokers experience a range of unpleasant mood and physical symptoms when they cannot smoke (see the next section, 3.4.3 Tobacco withdrawal syndrome). These symptoms can drive smokers back to cigarettes; depressed mood is of particular concern because it is unpleasant and also reduces the smoker's mental reserves needed to combat urges to smoke.

It is also thought that **another effect of nicotine** on the NAcc is to make the **activity of smoking**, and the stimuli that accompany it, **more rewarding** and pleasant, so that smokers come to like the feeling of smoke going into the throat and lungs and places and situations that usually accompany smoking – and they become attached to the particular look and taste of the brand that they smoke.

There are **psychological** and **social forces** at work which would not be enough in themselves to keep people smoking, but when combined with the effects of nicotine do seem to play an important role. Smokers think that smoking helps them **control stress**; they often find the **identity** of being a smoker more attractive than that of a non-smoker; and they get something out of the **camaraderie** of offering and receiving cigarettes. All of these things can make it more difficult for a smoker to stop.

Altogether, we must view **addiction to cigarettes** as involving **a number of forces** often working together: a **habit** that is built on the rewarding effect of nicotine in the midbrain; an **acquired drive**, somewhat like hunger, caused by nicotine modifying that midbrain system and associated brain structures; a **need to escape** from, or avoid, unpleasant effects of abstinence; and **social** and **psychological** factors that promote smoking. These forces lead the **smoker** to give an **unhealthy priority to smoking** that can easily overpower their desire not to smoke for the sake of their health or other reasons. Because some of these forces are outside the smoker's control and can affect people who normally have a strong will-power, we cannot see smoking just as a matter of choice – it involves a **psychological disorder of the motivational system** that threatens the smoker's life because of the diseases caused by smoking, but fortunately it **can be treated** (Box 3.2).

Box 3.2 Nicotine addiction.

Addiction involves a disorder of motivation which leads people to give an unhealthy priority to particular activities, usually involving taking some form of drug. This does not mean that addicts have no control at all over what they do, but it does make it difficult for them to abstain voluntarily.

Nicotine lies at the heart of addiction to cigarettes because it:

- Rewards smoking behaviour, thus creating a habit
- Changes the brain to create a kind of drive to smoke and unpleasant withdrawal symptoms when smokers abstain
- Makes the stimuli associated with smoking, including the feel of smoke going into the lungs, rewarding

3.4.3 Tobacco withdrawal syndrome

Tobacco withdrawal symptoms are **physical** and **mental changes** that occur following **interruption**, **reduction** or **termination** of **tobacco** use. They are **temporary** and are a product of physical or psychological adaptation to long-term tobacco use (in other words the smoker's mind and body gets used to having nicotine in their system), requiring a period of readjustment when tobacco is no longer used.

Stopping smoking usually brings on a **withdrawal syndrome**, comprising a **range of symptoms** (Table 3.3). It is the occurrence of these symptoms, especially urges to smoke, that leads to relapse early in a quit attempt (West et al., 1989a). However, **most withdrawal symptoms last no longer than 2–4 weeks** (West et al., 1989b; Hughes, 1992) and therefore assisting smokers through the first four weeks is important. Clients can be informed that withdrawal symptoms are due to them stopping smoking and not to any NRT that they may be using; and they can be reassured that these symptoms will pass, as long as they do not smoke.

More **severe urges to smoke** and **depression** are associated with a **greater risk of relapse**. There is no evidence that greater weight gain is associated with greater risk of relapse, in fact greater weight gain is related to lower risk of relapse. The statement box overleaf gives an example of what to say to a smoker about **withdrawal symptoms**.

Table 3.3 Tobacco withdrawal symptoms.

Symptom	Duration	Prevalence
Irritability/aggression	<4 weeks	50%
Depression	<4 weeks	60%
Restlessness	<4 weeks	60%
Poor concentration	<2 weeks	60%
Increased appetite	>10 weeks	70%
Light-headedness	<48 hours	10%
Night-time awakenings	<1 week	25%
Constipation	>4 weeks	17%
Mouth ulcers	>4 weeks	40%
Urges to smoke	>2 weeks	70%

A smoker's mind and body is used to regular doses of nicotine. When they stop smoking they go through a short period of readjustment where they experience withdrawal symptoms. As long as you do not have even one puff on a cigarette after your quit date these symptoms will gradually get easier to cope with and most will disappear within four weeks.

Withdrawal symptoms from chewing tobacco/dipping snuff are broadly similar to those from cigarettes, but probably less severe. Withdrawal symptoms from nicotine nasal spray, gum or other oral nicotine replacement products appear to be much less severe than from cigarettes and there is no evidence of withdrawal symptoms after cessation of nicotine patch use.

I am finding it difficult to concentrate, how long will this last?

It is fairly common for people to report this when they stop smoking. Difficulty in concentrating is a withdrawal symptom and as long as you do not smoke it typically gets better in a couple of weeks.

Smokers expect to feel physically better when they stop, but many report **feeling physically worse**. Many smokers report increased coughing, throat soreness, chest problems and mouth ulcers. The short-term decrease in salivary immunoglobulin A (part of the body's immune system), probably as a result of the stress involved with stopping smoking, may explain an increase in respiratory tract infections and mouth ulcers.

The special case of anxiety

- Many smokers report an increase in anxiety at the time of smoking cessation.
- It is beginning to look as though this is not a tobacco withdrawal symptom, but just a response to the act of trying to stop smoking.

How long do the withdrawal symptoms last?

Withdrawal symptoms are experienced by many, but not all, smokers when they stop. Most of these symptoms disappear within two to four weeks. Increased appetite can persist past four weeks. Urges to smoke may go on for a much longer time, but, as long as you do not smoke, they will become less frequent.

3.5 Treatment to help with stopping smoking

3.5.1 Principles of specialist treatment

NHS Stop Smoking Services were set up to provide specialist treatment for smokers wanting to stop; the staff at these services are specially trained and receiving treatment from them will **substantially increase** a smoker's **chances of quitting successfully** (West et al., 2000).

Most NHS Stop Smoking Services follow a similar structure: a **pre-quit** appointment for preparation, including the setting of a quit date, a **quit date** and **weekly appointments** up to at least **four weeks after the quit date**. This treatment focuses on preventing relapse in the early stages of a quit attempt by providing **intensive support** when withdrawal symptoms are at their worst, close **supervision of medication use**, and emphasising the importance of **complete abstinence**.

The key purpose of Stop Smoking Services is to provide clinical treatment to smokers who are planning to make a quit attempt and would like help with doing so. This service is generally provided by full-time specialist smoking cessation advisers and often in groups. Most services also provide community treatment to smokers. This treatment is provided by community advisers, typically, but not exclusively, community pharmacists or practice nurses, who deliver smoking cessation treatments on a part-time or sessional basis. An example of what to say to a smoker about **treatment** is shown in the statement box below.

There is strong evidence that getting help, support and advice in your quit attempt from someone specially trained in smoking cessation will roughly double your chances of success. Medications that help with stopping smoking have a similar effect and our local Stop Smoking Service can help you choose which medication is most suitable for you.

3.5.2 Types of medication

The only evidence-based medications that are available in the UK at present are **nicotine replacement therapy** (NRT) and **bupropion**

(Zyban). National Institute for Clinical Excellence (NICE) guidelines recommend that **nicotine replacement therapy** (NRT) or **bupropion** (Zyban) should be **offered to all smokers** who want to quit (NICE, 2002). Both medications are **effective** and **safe** to use. In the UK all medicines licensed for smoking cessation are **available on NHS prescription. NRT** is also available **over the counter** with some products on **general sale** (available in supermarkets and other retail outlets). The **most effective** treatment involves **medication** and **behavioural support**.

Nicotine replacement therapy (NRT)

For more information on NRT see Section 4.3.1 NRT.

For many smokers it is the urges to smoke and **depression** they experience at the start that lead to a **failed quit attempt**. NRT acts by providing a 'clean' alternative source of nicotine that the smoker would have otherwise received from tobacco. Nicotine delivered from NRT is absorbed more slowly and generally in a lesser amount than with cigarettes. It is, however, sufficient to **reduce the severity of these symptoms** and so can assist in maintaining abstinence.

There is now a large body of evidence that shows that NRT is **effective in helping smokers to quit**. The most recent systematic review of NRT studies concludes that it approximately **doubles the chance of long-term abstinence** compared to placebo and the odds of quitting are possibly even higher when more intensive support is provided (see Table 4.2).

How does NRT work?

Nicotine replacement therapy works by providing a small amount of nicotine that you would have otherwise received from your cigarettes. Since it is a smaller amount and not absorbed as fast as that from cigarettes it does not provide the same effect you get from smoking. However, it will reduce the withdrawal symptoms, including cravings, which many smokers experience when they stop. It will make your quit attempt a little easier and will improve your chances of success.

All NRT products provide a clean source of nicotine in a different way from smoking. There is **no difference** in the efficacy of the various **NRT products**, and little evidence for matching products to individual smokers. Therefore, it is generally agreed that choice of product can be guided by client preference. It is recommended that all products be **used for 8–12 weeks**.

An example of what to say to a smoker about **NRT** is shown in the statement box below.

> NRT, if used properly, gives you some of the nicotine that you get from cigarettes but in a different way. NRT helps to reduce the urges to smoke and discomfort (withdrawal symptoms) that smokers experience when they stop smoking and roughly doubles your chances of staying stopped.

Bupropion (Zyban)

For more information on Zyban see Section 4.3.2 Bupropion.

Bupropion (trade name **Zyban**) is an atypical antidepressant type medication that was also found by chance to help people stop smoking (note: at the doses at which it is prescribed for smoking cessation, and because of the length of time it is taken, bupropion does not act as an antidepressant). Research shows that this medication, like NRT, will **double smokers' chances of successfully stopping**. It is the only non-nicotine medication licensed for use in smoking cessation.

Bupropion works by reducing urges to smoke and other withdrawal symptoms once you have stopped smoking. Bupropion is **a relatively safe medicine** and is similar to many other antidepressants. Bupropion is **not suitable for everyone** to use and is only available on prescription.

How does Zyban work?

Exactly how Zyban works is not particularly clear, but we do know that it acts on parts of the brain where smoking has an effect. This helps by reducing the urges to smoke and other withdrawal symptoms, making quitting smoking a little easier.

The smoker needs to **start bupropion** about **one week** (strictly speaking 8 to 14 days) **before quitting**, allowing time for a steady state concentration to be reached. During this time they smoke as normal. Bupropion has some common side effects that include headache, dry mouth and difficulty sleeping. It also has a rare risk of seizure, estimated at less than 1 in 1000, which is similar to other antidepressants. The statement box overleaf gives an example of what to say to a smoker about **Zyban**.

Zyban can reduce the desire to smoke and is taken at least one week before your quit attempt, in order to build up to therapeutic levels. You will be asked to take one tablet for six days, whilst still smoking, and then increase to two tablets a day. A dry mouth and sleep disturbance are very common side effects, while a small proportion of people suffer more serious side effects such as seizures (fits). Zyban is relatively safe, but, because of the side effects, not everyone can take it. If you are one of these people then do not worry as you will be able to use NRT, which is as effective as Zyban and doesn't have any serious side effects.

3.5.3 Other treatments and interventions

There is **no evidence** that **hypnotherapy** or **acupuncture** increase smokers' chances of stopping successfully (White et al., 1999; Abbot et al., 2000).

There are a number of other products on the market that may be promoted as stop smoking aids. There are two, **clonidine** and **nortriptyline**, that have been demonstrated to help smokers but are not routinely used because they are associated with a number of side effects.

Does hypnotherapy or acupuncture work?

Some people report that they have found hypnotherapy or acupuncture useful. However, there is no evidence for the effectiveness of these methods in helping people stop smoking and your time, effort and money might be better used elsewhere.

Products such as Nicoblock, Nicobrevin and herbal cigarettes are not proven to help smokers stop and so cannot be recommended.

Self-help materials (leaflets and books) are a relatively inexpensive means of communicating cessation advice to a potentially large number of smokers. There is evidence that self-help materials **can help smokers to quit**, and that personalised materials may have an advantage over generic ones (Lancaster & Stead, 2002). Computer technology now offers the opportunity to personalise advice to smokers in a way that traditional written materials could not (Strecher, 1999). There appears to be no benefit of self-help materials when added to other brief interventions, but their effect may be enhanced when combined with more intensive interventions (Curry et al., 1995).

3.6 Referral to local services

Whether a smoker chooses to attend clinic treatment or community treatment will largely depend on the availability of the treatments and which they think they might prefer. Wherever a smoker lives in the UK there will be a **local NHS Stop Smoking Service near to them.** To find the local NHS Stop Smoking Service **smokers can telephone the NHS Smokers Helpline on 0800 169 0169** or visit **www.givingupsmoking.co.uk/nhs**

Most services accept, in fact prefer, clients who self refer. You could contact your local NHS Stop Smoking Service to confirm their referral arrangements. You may also be able to obtain promotional materials (for example posters, leaflets, referral cards) that you can use in your workplace.

Local contacts

Name of contact:	Service provided:	Contact details:

3.7 Wider context

In 1998 the UK Government announced its tobacco control strategy in the White Paper, *Smoking Kills* (Department of Health, 1998). As part of the package of measures, it announced the creation of a smoking cessation service funded by the NHS to assist smokers who want to stop, and which was responsible for the delivery of two levels of interventions. Smoking cessation guidelines that accompanied the White Paper emphasised that local services should be based on existing evidence and be organised around a core team of full-time specialist staff providing group smoking cessation treatment (level 3) (Raw et al., 1998). There was also to be a larger number of trained part-time community advisers, typically nurses working in primary care and community pharmacists, providing treatment one to one (level 2). Level 1 involved brief opportunistic smoking cessation advice from health professionals, specifically GPs, designed to stimulate quit attempts and to direct motivated smokers towards the local Stop Smoking Service.

The UK tobacco strategy is set out in a number of key documents shown in Table 3.4.

Table 3.4 Key documents forming the UK tobacco strategy.

Title	Strategy
Smoking Kills – A White Paper on Tobacco (*Department of Health,* December 1998)	Set out a comprehensive strategy to reduce tobacco smoking in the UK: ■ To reduce smoking among children from 13% to 9% or less by the year 2010 ■ To reduce adult smoking in all social classes so that the overall rate falls from 28% to 24% or less by the year 2010 ■ To reduce the percentage of women who smoke during pregnancy from 23% to 15% by the year 2010
Smoking cessation guidelines and their cost effectiveness: (West et al., 2000)	These documents set out the evidence base for the smoking cessation strategy outlined in the Tobacco White Paper and subsequent implementation.
NHS plan (Department of Health, 2000a)	Promised comprehensive smoking cessation services and NRT on prescription and re-emphasised importance of services for pregnant smokers.
NHS cancer plan (Department of Health, September 2000b)	Set new targets to reduce inequalities, including specific local targets for manual workers. Stressed importance of primary health care interventions and provided funding for local tobacco alliances and research; announced specific work to reduce smoking among ethnic minority groups.
Monitoring and service guidance (Department of Health, 2001)	Set out minimum standards for specialist smoking cessation services and good practice guidance on service provision and monitoring. ■ Specialist services must become part of core NHS activity ■ Specialist services must conform to minimum standards, involving offer of weekly support for up to four weeks after the quit date ■ Completion of monitoring forms is essential ■ All specialists must be trained to carry out their role

Table 3.4 (*continued*)

Title	Strategy
National priorities guidance 2003 to 2006 (Department of Health, December 2002a)	Identified smoking cessation as one of the Government's top priorities for the NHS, and set challenging targets for the NHS smoking cessation services.
Priorities and planning framework 2003–2006 (Department of Health, 2002b)	Set out the priorities for the NHS and social services and described what local organisations and communities need to do to plan for and implement the improvements. In the Cancer section: "Reduce the rate of smoking, contributing to the national target of: reducing the rate in manual groups from 32% in 1998 to 26% by 2010; 800 000 smokers from all groups successfully quitting at the four-week stage by 2006." In the Reducing health inequalities section: "Deliver a one percentage point reduction per year in the proportion of women continuing to smoke throughout pregnancy, focusing especially on smokers from disadvantaged groups as a contribution to the national target to reduce by at least 10% the gap in mortality between 'routine and manual' groups and the population as a whole by 2010, starting with children under one year." In the Coronary heart disease section: "In primary care, update practice-based registers so that clients with CHD and diabetes continue to receive appropriate advice and treatment in line with NSF standards and by March 2006, ensure practice-based registers and systematic treatment regimes, including appropriate advice on diet, physical activity and smoking, also cover the majority of clients at high risk of CHD, particular those with hypertension, diabetes and a BMI greater that 30."
Choosing health: making healthier choices easier (Public Health White Paper – 2004)	Set out the key principles for supporting the public to make healthier and more informed choices in regard to their health. Measures in relation to smoking: ■ Strengthening of legislation to ban retailers who sell tobacco products to children ■ By 2006 all Government departments and the NHS will be expected to be smoke-free ■ In 2005–6 the Healthcare Commission will examine what PCTs are doing to reduce smoking prevalence amongst the local population ■ Establish a national taskforce to increase the effectiveness and efficiency of NHS Stop Smoking Services ■ By 2008 all enclosed public places and workplaces will be smoke-free (exceptions: pubs and bars, other than restaurants, will be free to choose whether to allow smoking or to be smoke-free; in membership clubs the members will be free to choose whether to allow smoking or to be smoke-free; and smoking in the bar area will be prohibited everywhere)

Policy documents and useful Internet links relating to this topic are available on the website of the Smoking Cessation Service Research Network (SCSRN): www.scsrn.org

3.8 Multiple choice questions

Question 1: What percentage increase in smokers stopping for at least six months is achieved by GPs delivering brief advice?

- **a** 1–3%
- **b** 4–7%
- **c** 8–11%
- **d** 12–15%
- **e** 16–19%

Question 2: What is the most likely mechanism by which GP advice has its effect?

- **a** By scaring smokers
- **b** By increasing the chances of success of a quit attempt
- **c** By triggering a quit attempt
- **d** By providing a supportive environment
- **e** By the provision of nicotine replacement treatment

Question 3: Regarding brief advice, which of the following statements is FALSE?

- **a** It is effective when delivered by a GP
- **b** It can be delivered in just a few minutes
- **c** It should be documented in the patient notes that it was given
- **d** Its effectiveness is greater if it is provided more than six times a year
- **e** Brief advice delivered by other health care professionals has not yet been proven to be effective

Question 4: Regarding smoking status, which of the following statements is FALSE?

- **a** It should be checked as frequently as the health care professional deems appropriate
- **b** Asking about smoking status should be done in an appropriate way
- **c** Ex-smokers should be recorded as long-term (>12 months) or short-term (<12 months) ex-smokers
- **d** The date of change in smoking status should be recorded
- **e** It is not necessary to document if a patient has never smoked

Question 5: Regarding the provision of brief advice, which of the following statements is FALSE?

- **a** It should only be provided to those smokers who show some interest in stopping
- **b** It should contain some positive messages
- **c** It should be documented that it has been provided
- **d** Smokers may be more receptive if this is linked with an existing medical condition
- **e** A good opportunity to give brief advice is during routine consultation

Question 6: Regarding assessment of readiness to quit and provision of treatment, which of the following statements is FALSE?

- **a** Smokers will generally fall into one of three categories: do not want to stop; do not want to stop at this time; do want to stop.
- **b** Information about using NRT to cut down to quit in the near future can be provided to those who do not want to stop, or are not interested in quitting at this time
- **c** For those smokers who want to quit, they should be referred to the local Stop Smoking Services wherever possible
- **d** For those smokers who want to quit but do not want to go to the local Stop Smoking Service, treatment can be provided by a primary health care professional
- **e** Smokers not wanting to stop can be advised to switch to a lower tar cigarette

Question 7: Regarding recording the advice given and responses, which of the following statements is FALSE?

- **a** For those who do not want to stop smoking they should be given further advice to quit within the next 12 months
- **b** For those who wish to quit, the outcome of the advice should be recorded
- **c** Those smokers who make a quit attempt should be asked at the next meeting how this quit attempt went
- **d** If a smoker is not interested in quitting this should be recorded so that the GP does not make the mistake of giving advice to quit again
- **e** The Read code for the provision of smoking cessation advice is 8CAL

Question 8: Regarding cutting down, which of the following statements is FALSE?

- **a** Cutting down unaided is not a recommended way to stop smoking
- **b** A smoker who cuts down from 20 to 10 cigarettes per day is likely to receive significantly less nicotine
- **c** Low tar cigarettes are not a healthier option
- **d** Cutting down with nicotine replacement therapy can avoid compensatory smoking
- **e** Smokers can compensate for a lower cigarette consumption by smoking the remaining cigarettes more intensively

Question 9: Regarding the neurobiology of nicotine dependence, which of the following statements is FALSE?

- **a** Nicotine binds to dopamine receptors in the ventral tegmental area
- **b** Smoking results in dopamine release in the nucleus accumbens
- **c** Dopamine release in the nucleus accumbens is important in rewarding behaviour
- **d** Acetylcholine is a neurotransmitter
- **e** Smokers do not need to feel pleasure when smoking a cigarette for 'nicotine reward' to occur

Question 10: Regarding nicotine, which of the following statements is FALSE?

- **a** Nicotine rewards smoking, causing the behaviour to be repeated
- **b** Nicotine changes the brain to create unpleasant withdrawal symptoms when smokers abstain
- **c** After 24 hours urges to smoke are reduced
- **d** Nicotine readily crosses the blood-brain barrier
- **e** Nicotine from cigarette smoke reaches the brain within 20 seconds

Question 11: Which of the following is not a tobacco withdrawal symptom?

- **a** Irritability
- **b** Restlessness
- **c** Headache
- **d** Poor concentration
- **e** Increased appetite

Question 12: Regarding tobacco withdrawal symptoms, which of the following statements is FALSE?

- **a** Most last less than four weeks
- **b** Urges to smoke can lead to relapse early in the quit attempt
- **c** Helping smokers get through the first few weeks of a quit attempt is important
- **d** Increased weight gain is associated with an increased risk of relapse
- **e** Withdrawal symptoms may appear after discontinuing the use of nicotine nasal spray or chewing gum

Question 13: Regarding mouth ulcers, which of the following statements is TRUE?

- **a** Mouth ulcers are usually a side effect of nicotine chewing gum
- **b** Occurrence may be related to the short-term decrease in salivary immunoglobulin-A
- **c** Mouth ulcers occur in less than 10% of smokers who make a quit attempt
- **d** Mouth ulcers last for less than four weeks
- **e** Smokers who experience mouth ulcers are more likely to relapse

Question 14: Regarding light-headedness, which of the following statements is FALSE?

- **a** Light-headedness is experienced by approximately 10% of clients
- **b** Light-headedness lasts less than 48 hours on average
- **c** Light-headedness is part of the nicotine withdrawal syndrome
- **d** Clients can be reassured that light-headedness will soon pass
- **e** Light-headedness is likely to be due to the client receiving too much nicotine from their NRT product

Question 15: Regarding treatment received from the Stop Smoking Service, which of the following statements is FALSE?

- **a** Treatment approximately doubles the chance of long-term success
- **b** Treatment typically involves setting a quit date and weekly appointments for four weeks after this
- **c** Treatment is generally provided by full-time specialist smoking cessation advisers
- **d** Treatment generally achieves long-term quit rates of less than 10%
- **e** Treatment might be delivered by pharmacists and practice nurses who have been specially trained

Question 16: Regarding nicotine replacement treatments and bupropion, which of the following statements is FALSE?

- **a** They are proven effective
- **b** They are recommended as first line treatments for tobacco dependence
- **c** They are both available over the counter
- **d** They roughly double the chances of successfully quitting
- **e** They should be offered to all smokers who want to quit

Question 17: Regarding NRT, which of the following statements is FALSE?

- **a** It provides only nicotine
- **b** Nicotine from NRT is absorbed as quickly as that from cigarettes
- **c** It typically provides less nicotine than smoking
- **d** There are no differences in the efficacy of the various NRT products
- **e** It should be used for 8–12 weeks

Question 18: Regarding bupropion, which of the following statements is TRUE?

- **a** It is an anxiolytic drug
- **b** It is one of three non-nicotine medications licensed for smoking cessation
- **c** It is available on prescription
- **d** It is started on quit day
- **e** It has a risk of seizure of 1 in 100

Question 19: Regarding other treatments for smoking cessation, which of the following statements is TRUE?

- **a** Hypnosis is effective for smoking cessation
- **b** Acupuncture is effective for smoking cessation
- **c** Nortriptyline is effective for smoking cessation, but is not routinely used
- **d** Clonidine has few side effects
- **e** Nicobrevin can be recommended to smokers who do not wish to use bupropion

Question 20: Key components of smoking cessation treatment include all but which one of the following?

- **a** Multi-session behavioural support
- **b** Use of NRT and bupropion
- **c** Supervision of medication use
- **d** Emphasis on the importance of complete abstinence
- **e** Lecturing on the risks of smoking

References

Abbot, N.C., Stead, L.F., White, A.R., Barnes, J. & Ernst, E. (2000). Hypnotherapy for smoking cessation. *Cochrane Database of Systematic Reviews*, (2), CD001008.

Benowitz, N., Jacob, P., Kozlowski, L. & Yu, L. (1986). Influence of smoking fewer cigarettes on exposure to tar, nicotine and carbon monoxide. *New England Journal of Medicine*, *315* (21), 1310–1313.

Butler, C.C., Pill, R. & Stott, N.C. (1998). Qualitative study of patients' perceptions of doctors' advice to quit smoking: implications for opportunistic health promotion. *British Medical Journal*, *316* (7148), 1878–1881.

Curry, S.J., McBride, C., Grothaus, L.C., Louie, D. & Wagner, E.H. (1995). A randomised trial of self-help materials, personalised feedback and telephone counselling with non-volunteer smokers. *Journal of Consulting and Clinical Psychology*, *63* (6), 1005–1014.

Department of Health (1998). *Smoking Kills: A White Paper on Tobacco*. London: The Stationery Office.

Department of Health (2000a). *The NHS Plan: Command Paper 4818–1*. London: Department of Health.

Department of Health (2000b). *The NHS Cancer Plan: a Plan for Investment, a Plan for Reform*. London: Department of Health.

Department of Health (2001). *NHS Smoking Cessation Services: Service and Monitoring Cessation Services: Service and Monitoring Guidance. 2001/02*. London: Department of Health.

Department of Health (2002a). *Improvement, Expansion and Reform – the Next Three Years: Priorities and Planning Framework 2003–2006*. London: Department of Health.

Department of Health (2002b). *Priorities and Planning Framework 2003–2006: Improvement, Expansion and Reform*. London: Department of Health.

Department of Health (2004). *Choosing Health: Making Healthier Choices Easier*. London: Department of Health.

Hughes, J.R. (1992). Tobacco withdrawal in self-quitters. *Journal of Consulting and Clinical Psychology*, *60* (5), 689–697.

Lancaster, T. & Stead, L.F. (2002). Self-help interventions for smoking cessation. *Cochrane Database of Systematic Reviews*, (3), CD001118.

McEwen, A. & West, R. (2001). Smoking cessation activities by general practitioners and practice nurses. *Tobacco Control*, *10* (1), 27–32.

National Institute for Clinical Excellence (2002). *Guidance on the Use of Nicotine Replacement Therapy (NRT) and Bupropion for Smoking Cessation*. London: National Institute for Clinical Excellence.

Office for National Statistics (2004). *Living in Britain – the 2002 General Household Survey*. London: Office for National Statistics.

Raw, M., McNeill, A. & West, R. (1998). Smoking cessation guidelines for health professionals. A guide to effective smoking cessation interventions for the health care system. Health Education Authority. *Thorax*, *53* (Suppl. 5 Pt 1), S1–19.

Silagy, C. (2000). Physician advice for smoking cessation. *Cochrane Database of Systematic Reviews*, (2), CD000165.

Strecher, V.J. (1999). Computer-tailored smoking cessation materials: a review and discussion. *Patient Education and Counselling*, *36* (2), 107–117.

USDHHS (2000). *Treating Tobacco Use and Dependence*. Rockville, Md.: Agency for Healthcare Research Quality.

West, R.J., Hajek, P. & Belcher, M. (1989a). Severity of withdrawal symptoms as a predictor of outcome of an attempt to quit smoking. *Psychological Medicine*, *19* (4), 981–985.

West, R., Hajek, P. & Belcher, M. (1989b). Time course of cigarette withdrawal symptoms while using nicotine gum. *Psychopharmacology (Berlin)*, *99* (1), 143–145.

West, R. & McEwen, A. (1999). *Sex and Smoking: Comparisons between Male and Female Smokers*. London: No Smoking Day.

West, R., McNeill, A. & Raw, M. (2000). National smoking cessation guidelines for health professionals: an update. *Thorax*, *55*, 987–999.

West, R. (2006). Defining and assessing nicotine dependence in humans. Novartis Foundation Symposium, May 2005. In: Goode, J. (Ed) *Understanding Smoking and Nicotine Addiction*. London: Wiley.

White, A.R., Resch, K.L. & Ernst, E. (1999). A meta-analysis of acupuncture techniques for smoking cessation. *Tobacco Control*, *8* (4), 393–397.

Chapter 4

Intensive one-to-one support and advice

This chapter provides information necessary for health professionals to provide intensive one-to-one interventions with smokers. It could be that such interventions are delivered by full-time smoking cessation specialists, or by community advisers (CAs): health care professionals who deliver smoking cessation treatment one to one with clients on a sessional or part-time basis. It is anticipated that health professionals intending to deliver such interventions to smokers will have an understanding of the information in Part One (Chapters 1 and 2) of this manual. It is also expected that they will have read, and will use, the knowledge and skills required to deliver brief advice (Chapter 3) and that they have attended a specialist training course (HDA, 2002).

4.1 Smoking cessation treatments and their outcome

It has been the intention that NHS Stop Smoking Services, where possible, will deliver **evidence-based treatment** to maximise the chances of success of those clients attending for treatment. In fact, the first ever national, evidence-based guidelines on smoking cessation activities for health professionals (Raw et al., 1998) formed the basis for the chapter on cessation in the Government White Paper, *Tobacco Kills* (Department of Health, 1998).

4.1.1 Evaluation of smoking cessation methods

The effectiveness of smoking cessation methods are reported in various ways. For example Table 4.2 uses **effect size**: the **difference in abstinence rates** between the intervention and control/placebo groups for at least six months post quit. So, if 2% of smokers who attend a GP surgery, and do not receive any advice, quit smoking long-term, 4% of those who are advised to stop by their GP will stop as a result of this advice. Sometimes the effectiveness of treatment is presented as an **odds ratio**: the **odds of long-term abstinence** of one treatment compared with another. A result over one means that the treatment increases the odds of abstinence, below one that the odds of success are reduced. For example, the overall odds ratio for long-term abstinence with NRT, irrespective of additional support, compared to placebo has an odds ratio (OR) of 1.77 (Silagy et al., 2004). There are also a number of ways in which abstinence is assessed as shown in Table 4.1.

Table 4.1 Examples of how abstinence is assessed.

Evaluation	Description	Comment
Self-report	Smoking status established by client reporting whether or not they are still smoking (face to face or via telephone, email, Internet or post).	This has the obvious disadvantage of 'allowing' clients to report being a non-smoker when they are still smoking.
CO validated	This 'validates' self-report by chemically verifying smoking status (see Section 4.2.4). Knowing that there will be validation increases the reliability of self-report.	Requires face-to-face contact and, because of the half-life of CO, only really confirms that client has not smoked in previous 24 hours.
Cotinine validated	This metabolite of nicotine can be assessed from a saliva, urine or blood sample and 'validates' self-report.	Cotinine has a longer half-life than CO and so it is a more reliable marker of abstinence and can assess smoking in the last week. However, it cannot distinguish between nicotine from a cigarette and that from NRT. It requires face-to-face contact, sample collection and costs about £10 per sample to analyse.
Point prevalence	Abstinence, self-reported or CO validated, for (usually) one week prior to follow-up point.	This is likely to overestimate abstinence rates as 'allows' for significant periods of time smoking between assessment points.
Continuous abstinence	Abstinence, self-reported or CO validated, continuously between quit date and follow-up point.	This is probably the best measure of long-term abstinence but does not 'allow' for clients who have a lapse but fully re-establish abstinence.

4.1.2 Short-term treatment outcomes

The Russell Standard (Clinical) is probably the best compromise between practicability and rigour when evaluating the success of NHS Stop Smoking Services (West, 2005a). It is designed to clarify the requirements set out in the Department of Health monitoring guidance (Department of Health, 2001), and is summarised in Box 4.1.

Box 4.1 Department of Health Monitoring Guidance.

The criteria

(1) A 'treated smoker' (TS) is a smoker who undergoes at least one treatment session on or prior to the quit date and sets a firm quit date. Smokers who attend an assessment session but fail to attend thereafter would not be counted. Neither are smokers who have already stopped smoking at the time they first come to the attention of the services. Smokers who have quit spontaneously within the past two weeks and seek and receive help from the service can also be counted but should be noted separately as they will naturally have higher success rates.

(2) A smoker is counted as a 'self-reported four-week quitter' (SR4WQ) if s/he is a 'treated smoker', is assessed (face to face, by postal questionnaire or by telephone) four weeks after the designated quit date (minus three days or plus fourteen days) and declares that s/he has not smoked even a single puff on a cigarette in the past two weeks. In smokers who quit up to two weeks prior to seeking help, their own prior quit date is the 'designated quit date'.

Russell Standard (Clinical)

(1) A smoker is counted as a 'CO-verified 4-week quitter' (4WQ) if s/he is a self-reported four-week quitter and his/her expired-air CO is assessed four weeks after the designated quit date (minus three days or plus fourteen days) and found to be less than 10 ppm.

(2) A treated smoker is counted as 'lost to follow-up at four weeks' (LFU4W) if, on attempting to determine the four-week quitter status s/he cannot be contacted.

(3) A smoker is counted as a '52-week quitter' (52WQ) if s/he is a 'treated smoker', is assessed (face to face, by postal questionnaire or by telephone) 52 weeks after the designated quit date (plus or minus 30 days) and declares that s/he has not smoked more than five cigarettes in the past 50 weeks.

(4) A treated smoker is counted as 'lost to follow-up at 52 weeks' (LFU52W) if, on attempting to determine the 52-week quitter status s/he cannot be contacted.

Calculating success rates

(1) The four-week success rate (4WSR) is 4WQ/TS. This will generally be above 40%.

(2) The self-reported four-week success rate (SR4WSR) is SR4WQ/TS. This will generally be above 50%.

(3) The 52-week success rate (52WSR) is 52WQ/TS. This will generally be at least 15%.

Smoking cessation services report four-week abstinence rates of, on average, 53%, validated by expired-air carbon monoxide (Bauld et al., 2003).

4.1.3 Long-term treatment outcomes

One user in seven (14.6%) reported continued abstinence and was CO validated as a successful quitter at 52 weeks in a review of English NHS Stop Smoking Services (Ferguson et al., 2005). See Table 4.2.

If I go to one of the clinics, how likely is it that they will help me stop smoking?	*Getting treatment from a Stop Smoking Clinic is the most effective way to stop smoking. At the end of treatment over half of clients are successfully off cigarettes; and this includes very heavy smokers who often have never managed to stop for a single week before.*

4.1.4 Relapse

Relapse back to smoking is, in one sense, part and parcel of nicotine dependence. "**Every smoker who quits remains prone to relapse**" (Piasecki, 2002). The survival curve in Figure 4.1 shows that the risk

Figure 4.1 Survival curve for a typical unaided attempt to stop smoking.

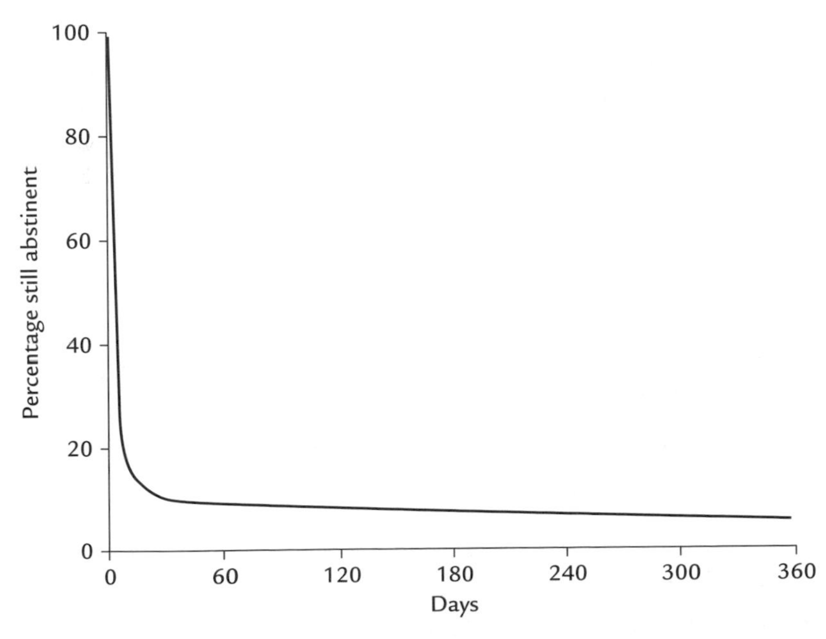

West & Shiffman, 2004

Table 4.2 Incremental effects of smoking cessation interventions on abstinence for six months or longer.

Intervention	Target population	Effect size[1]	95% Confidence Interval[2]
Brief opportunistic advice from a physician to stop	Smokers attending GP surgeries or outpatient clinics	2%	1–3%
Face-to-face intensive behavioural support from a specialist[3]	Moderate to heavy smokers seeking help with stopping	7%	3–10%
Face-to-face intensive behavioural support from a specialist	Pregnant smokers	7%	5–9%
Face-to-face intensive behavioural support from a specialist[4]	Smokers admitted to hospital	4%	0–8%
Pro-active telephone counselling[5]	Smokers wanting help with stopping but not receiving face-to-face support	2%	1–4%
Written self-help materials	Smokers seeking help with stopping	1%	0–2%
Nicotine gum	Moderate to heavy smokers receiving *limited*[6] behavioural support	5%	4–6%
Nicotine gum	Moderate to heavy smokers receiving *intensive* behavioural support	8%	6–10%
Nicotine transdermal patch	Moderate to heavy smokers receiving *limited* behavioural support	5%	4–7%
Nicotine transdermal patch	Moderate to heavy smokers receiving *intensive* behavioural support	6%	5–8%
Nicotine nasal spray	Moderate to heavy smokers receiving *intensive* behavioural support	12%	7–17%
Nicotine inhalator	Moderate to heavy smokers receiving *intensive* behavioural support	8%	4–12%
Nicotine sublingual tablet	Moderate to heavy smokers receiving *intensive* behavioural support	8%	1–14%
Bupropion (300 mg pd SR)	Moderate to heavy smokers receiving *intensive* behavioural support	9%	5–14%
Intensive behavioural support plus NRT or bupropion[7]	Moderate to heavy smokers seeking help from a clinic	13–19%	—

1 Difference in >6 month abstinence rate between intervention and control/placebo in the studies reported; data from Cochrane meta-analyses unless otherwise stated.
2 The range within which one can be 95% confident that the true underlying value lies.
3 Efficacy figures based on subset of studies from general population with biochemical verification.
4 No Cochrane review available, data from USDHHS meta-analysis.
5 No Cochrane review available, data from USDHHS meta-analysis.
6 The term 'limited behavioural support' refers to brief sessions required primarily for collecting data. Following the Cochrane definition, 'intensive behavioural support' was defined as an initial session of more than 30 minutes, or an initial session of less than 30 minutes plus more than two subsequent visits.
7 Expected effect combining effect of medication with effect of behavioural support.

West et al., 2000

for relapse is greatest early on in the quit attempt, with a very sharp drop-off in the first week. By two to three months, the risk is considerably reduced, and most (but by no means all) smokers who have remained abstinent for that period are likely to become lifelong ex-smokers.

A working definition is that a **lapse** is one, or a few, cigarettes followed by a **resumption of the quit attempt**. A **relapse** is the **resumption of regular smoking**, even if at a lower level.

The occasions of acute **stress** and when smokers' **barriers are down** appear to be when quitters lapse (see Box 4.2). Broadly speaking **relapse** is associated with circumstances (situations or emotional states) that promote relapse by:

(1) **Evoking craving**

(2) **Increasing motivation to smoke**

(3) **Weakening resolve to abstain**

(4) **Making cigarettes easier to obtain**

Box 4.2 High-risk relapse situations.

Situations when clients report **acute stress** as a reason for returning to smoking are more often than not:

- Arguments with partners or family
- When the pressure is on at work
- Christmas
- Bereavement

Barriers to relapsing back to smoking appear to be **reduced** when clients are:

- Under the influence of alcohol
- On holiday
- In the company of smokers in a smoking permissive environment.

There is a **lack of evidence** to support the use of any specific **relapse prevention interventions**, although there is limited methodologically sound research on this topic. Until more evidence becomes available it may be more efficient to focus on supporting the initial cessation attempt than on additional relapse prevention efforts (Hajek et al.,

Box 4.3 Unproven strategies that might prevent relapse.

Self-help strategies:

- 'Relapse' back onto NRT. Suggest that clients keep oral NRT with them and use this before smoking a cigarette when tempted.
- Identify risky situations. Anticipating high-risk situations and planning to avoid or deal with them may raise the personal priority of remaining abstinent.
- Maintain morale. A client reminding him/herself about the reasons they wanted to stop smoking, the things they disliked about smoking and the benefits of stopping (including health and monetary gains) may bolster motivation.
- Active strategies. Taking exercise, telephoning a 'buddy' or help-line, or doing something to take 'their minds off it' could all be useful.

Help from Stop Smoking Services:

- Provision of oral NRT products for client to 'relapse' onto if needed.
- Advice and assistance on high-risk situations and coping skills.
- Information on ongoing support. Provision of cards with useful telephone numbers.
- Support group. Open meetings held regularly for clients feeling vulnerable to relapse, or approaching a high-risk situation, to attend to maintain morale and be reminded of active strategies.
- 'Top-up' appointments. Regular, though less frequent than weekly, support groups that attempt to prolong the treatment effect.

2005). The strategies shown in Box 4.3 are incorporated into many NHS Stop Smoking Services and there is a need for them to be properly evaluated.

4.2 Assessment

4.2.1 Nicotine dependence

The level of **nicotine dependence** should be **assessed** to enable the provision of **appropriate treatment** and to set **success rates** in the context of the **type of smokers** being treated. The number of cigarettes smoked per day is not a strong indicator of how dependent a smoker is. Furthermore, smokers can compensate for a lesser number of cigarettes smoked per day (see Section 3.3.2). A simple and reliable way to measure dependence is to ask: "**How soon after waking do you smoke the first cigarette of the day?**" If a smoker

Figure 4.2 Fagerström test for nicotine dependence (FTND).

	Circle one response	
How many cigarettes per day do you usually smoke?	10 or less	0
	11 to 20	1
	21 to 30	2
	31 or more	3
How soon after you wake up do you smoke your first cigarette?	Within 5 minutes	3
	6–30 minutes	2
	More than 30 minutes	1
Do you find it difficult to stop smoking in no-smoking areas?	No	0
	Yes	1
Which cigarette would you most hate to give up?	The first of the morning	1
	Other	0
Do you smoke more frequently in the first hours after waking than during the rest of the day?	No	0
	Yes	1
Do you smoke if you are so ill that you are in bed most of the day?	No	0
	Yes	1

smokes **within 30 minutes** of waking, they are a **more dependent** smoker and would benefit from **more intensive smoking cessation treatment** and **higher dose medication**. This question is taken from the Fagerström test for nicotine dependence (FTND) (Heatherton et al., 1991); in research the full set of questions is usually used when assessing dependence. The full version is reproduced in Figure 4.2, and the column on the right indicates how responses should be scored. The higher the score the more dependent a smoker is (the maximum score is 10). Clients attending NHS Stop Smoking Clinics score about 5.5 on average.

You may come across examples of where FTND scores are categorised (for example 0–2 = very low dependence, 8–10 = very high dependence); these arbitrary groupings are not necessarily very useful and it is best to think of dependence as a scale (0–10) rather than as distinct categories.

4.2.2 Interest in quitting and willingness to attend for treatment

As already mentioned in Chapter 3 (Section 3.2.2 Assessment of interest in quitting) the simplest way of determining whether a client is interested in stopping smoking is to **ask them**. Once this is established it is important to determine that if they wish to get behavioural support during their quit attempt, they are willing and able to attend the treatment appointments. The statement box below gives an example of assessing a **client's willingness to attend for treatment**.

I am pleased that you would like to stop smoking and that you would like to see me so that I can help you with this. Regular attendance at appointments is important and so perhaps we can now both check our diaries to make sure that you are able to make the remaining appointments over the next few weeks.

The Stages of change model (or the Transtheoretical model) (DiClemente et al., 1991) is used by some services to assess motivation to quit in clients, but has not been found in research to improve on a simple common-sense approach. The limitations of the model are explored in more detail elsewhere (see for example, Sutton, 2001; West, 2005b), but Box 4.4 provides a summary.

Box 4.4 Limitations of Stages of change (SOC) model.

The model draws **arbitrary dividing lines** in order to differentiate the stages, and this must mean that these are not really discrete stages. For example, an individual who is planning to stop smoking is in the preparation stage if this is within the next 30 days, but only the contemplation stage if it is in 31 days' time.

In **addition**, in focusing on stages defined in terms of when the quit is supposed to take place, it **neglects** important underpinnings of human motivation: the role of reward and punishment in developing **habits** that are hard to break; the importance of associations as **triggers** to feelings and actions; the **immediate** impact of **barriers** and **facilitators** of change.

The model really says no more than that individuals who are thinking of changing their behaviour are more likely at follow-up to have changed their behaviour than those who are not, or that individuals who are in the process of trying to change their behaviour are more likely to change than those who are just thinking about it. Put that way, it is **just a statement of the obvious**: people who want or plan to do something are obviously more likely to try to do it; and people who try to do something are more likely to succeed than those who do not. This simple account is far from adequate. Research shows that immediate triggers play a very important role in behaviour change. It also shows that the model is outperformed in the case of smoking by an 'addiction' model.

Where interventions have been developed that are based on the model these have **not** proved **more effective** than interventions which are based on **traditional concepts**. A recent review comparing stop smoking interventions designed using the SOC approach with non-tailored treatments found no benefit for those based on the model. On the other hand, there is good evidence that tailoring interventions in other ways, including triggers and motives are more effective than untailored approaches.

Adapted from West, 2005b

The Stages of change model should not be used because it:

(1) Makes the assessment of readiness to quit more complex and involved than is necessary

(2) May provoke the wrong intervention strategy

(3) Is likely to lead to effective interventions not being offered to people who would have responded

4.2.3 Smoking characteristics

We have already seen in Chapter 1 (Section 1.2 Smoking cessation) that **cessation rates** are **lower** for **more dependent smokers**, in **more deprived socio-economic groups** and among those with **lower educational levels. Young smokers** are **less** likely to be **successful** in attempts to stop smoking. The **chances of success** of quit attempts are also **lower** in those who **live with smokers** versus non-smokers, and those who **live alone** versus with a partner. Spending more **time in the company of smokers** appears to be related to **lower success rates**, but having managed to go a **long time without smoking in recent years** has been shown to be positively related to **success.** Clients with these negative prognostic signs may need **more intensive help** (for example telephone contact between sessions, higher dose NRT or combinations of medications). The questions listed in Figure 4.3 are suggestions for determining a client's quitting history and past medication use. These may inform your discussions about medication with clients and the questions can be asked in questionnaire form (as below) or during the initial conversation with clients.

Figure 4.3 Assessing quitting history.

(1)	Have you made a serious attempt to stop smoking before? (*Circle 'No' or write the number of times in the space.*)	No Yes...............times
(2)	What is the longest that a quit attempt has lasted in the past? (*Write the number of months, days or weeks in the box – please specify which.*)	[ ]
(3)	Have you ever used nicotine replacement treatment in the past? (*Please circle.*)	Yes No
(4)	Have you ever used Zyban in the past? (*Please circle.*)	Yes No

The statement box below gives an example of responding to client's answers to questions determining quitting history and past medication use.

I see that you have tried to stop smoking a number of times before and that you have never lasted more than a couple of weeks. Having tried and failed to stop in the past does not harm your chances of quitting successfully this time, and having gone a few weeks without smoking, when the withdrawal symptoms are at their strongest, shows that you can do it.

The question in Figure 4.4 suggests means of assessing reasons for quitting that may inform your discussions with clients.

Figure 4.4 Assessing reasons for quitting.

Why do you want to give up smoking? (*Circle the most important reason.*)	
	■ Because my health is already suffering
	■ Because I am worried about my future health
	■ Because smoking costs too much
	■ Because other people are pressurising me to
	■ For my family's health

4.2.4 Carbon monoxide monitoring

Carbon monoxide (CO) is one of the constituents of cigarette smoke and when inhaled it takes the **place of oxygen** on haemoglobin contained in the **red blood cells**. CO is linked to coronary heart disease and is associated with adverse effects in pregnancy. **CO** is an approximate **indicator** of how much **a smoker has smoked**. However, CO is eliminated from the body fairly quickly (in about 24 hours) and so if a client has **not smoked** since their quit date then their CO reading should be **below 10 ppm** (parts per million) or less than 7 ppm above the ambient (room) CO reading. An example of explaining CO monitoring is shown in the statement box below.

Carbon monoxide (CO) is one of the things that you inhale when you smoke cigarettes; it takes the place of oxygen in your red blood cells and contributes to coronary heart disease. The good news is that if you do not smoke after your quit date then your carbon monoxide levels will drop to that of a non-smoker.

Whilst you are still smoking I would expect your CO levels to be fairly high (depending upon what time of the day we measure your CO), but once you have quit it should drop below 10 ppm. I will measure your CO levels every time I see you with this CO monitor. This will let me know whether you have been smoking and also provide you with a good indication that, however you may be feeling, your health is already improving. ”

A CO monitor is an important piece of equipment to have for treating smokers. It not only **verifies** that clients are **not smoking**, but is also a useful **motivational tool**. Smokers like to see the change in CO when they stop smoking, and this is one of few objective initial health benefits of quitting that they will have evidence of. A CO monitor is also useful for confirming abstinence before supplying more medications (see Box 4.5 and Section 4.3.4 below).

Box 4.5 Important points to remember about CO monitoring.

- CO monitoring is not a breath test; it measures the amount of CO in **expired air**, which gives an indication of the level contained in blood.
- It is important that clients **hold their breath** for **10–15 seconds** (or for as long as they can if this is difficult) prior to exhaling into the CO monitor. This allows the levels of CO in the blood to equalise with the air in the lungs.
- CO readings are **rarely zero** as the body produces small amounts itself and there is CO in the atmosphere.
- CO **builds up in the body** throughout the day and so in smokers a reading in the morning is likely to be lower than if the CO test is done later on in the day.
- People who **do not smoke** will generally have a reading of between **3–6 ppm** and certainly less than 10 ppm.
- CO readings will not continue to fall week by week, but once the client has stopped smoking it will remain below 10 ppm.
- Inhaling other people's cigarette smoke does not normally push the reading over 10 ppm if the client is not smoking.

Why doesn't my CO reading get lower each week?

Our bodies produce small amounts of CO and of course there is CO in the air as well, so your CO will never be zero. You CO reading may fluctuate because of this from week to week, but as long as you do not smoke it will remain below 10 ppm and you will be 'classed' as a non-smoker.

There are a number of reasons why a client can have a **CO** reading **above 10 ppm** after their quit date, the most obvious being that they have **smoked**. However, if they did not have a cigarette then a high CO reading could be due to a **faulty car exhaust**, long periods working with **paint stripper**, or a **faulty gas boiler**. In such circumstances confrontation can be avoided using the suggested example below. Some people are **lactose intolerant** (unable to effectively digest the main sugar in milk) and this can result in raised levels of hydrogen in their breath. The cells in some CO monitors are unable to distinguish between hydrogen and CO and this can result in high readings. However, most people are aware of their lactose intolerance because of other symptoms (nausea, cramps, bloating, gas and diarrhoea, which begin about 30 minutes to two hours after eating or drinking foods containing lactose) and this should be easy to establish as a reason for high CO readings. The statement box below gives an example of advising clients about raised CO levels **when they claim that they have not smoked**.

The most common reason for raised CO levels after the quit date is that the person has smoked. However, there are some other possible reasons, such as leaking car exhausts, faulty gas boilers and working with some paint strippers. I would suggest that in the coming week you get your exhaust and gas boiler checked so that when you come back next week, not having smoked, you should have a nice low CO reading.

4.3 Pharmacotherapy

4.3.1 Nicotine replacement therapy (NRT)

There is now a large body of evidence that shows that NRT is **effective in helping smokers to quit**. The most recent systematic review of

NRT studies concludes that it approximately **doubles the chance of long-term abstinence** compared to placebo (Silagy et al., 2004) and the odds of quitting are possibly even higher when more intensive support is provided (Sutherland, 2003) (see Table 4.2).

Is NRT safe?

Yes, NRT is safe to use. It contains only nicotine that you would have otherwise received from cigarettes and not the other harmful constituents of tobacco smoke. NRT typically provides a smaller amount of nicotine, more slowly, than cigarettes. Remember, it is not nicotine that causes the health problems associated with smoking but the other things such as tar and carbon monoxide.

All NRT products provide a 'clean' source of nicotine in a different way from smoking. There is no evidence for difference in the efficacy of the various NRT products overall, and little evidence for matching products to individual smokers. Therefore, it is generally agreed that choice of product can be guided by client preference. However, **more dependent smokers** benefit more from a **higher dose** or **faster acting product**, such as 4 mg gum, or 4 mg lozenge, or nasal spray (West & Shiffman, 2004). It is recommended that all products be **used for 8–12 weeks**; but clients may **need** to take it for **longer**.

Nicotine transdermal patch

The nicotine patch is one of the most commonly used NRT products. It is available in **16-hour** and **24-hour** preparations, both releasing approximately 1 mg of nicotine per hour. Current evidence shows **no difference in efficacy** between the two, which means that choice of patch can be guided by **client preference**. Patches are also available in lower strengths designed for 'weaning off'; although there is no evidence to suggest that this is absolutely necessary.

The advantage of patches is that they are very **simple to use** and there is generally **good adherence** to treatment. They are applied to a clean, dry and hairless area of skin in the morning and removed at the end of the day (16 hr), or the next morning (24 hr). A possible disadvantage of the patch is the **slow nicotine delivery**, which means that it cannot be used to combat acute surges in craving. Time taken to reach plateau concentrations varies between two and eight hours depending on the particular brand. Skin irritation is the most common side effect. The 24-hour patch may cause sleep disturbance (also a withdrawal symptom) and vivid dreams.

Should I use the 16 or 24-hour patch?

The choice is really up to you. Both patches provide nicotine at the same rate and there is no difference in their effectiveness. Some people like the thought of patches providing them with nicotine overnight so they have some in their system when they wake up in the morning. Others like to have a break from nicotine whilst they are sleeping. Remember, both types will double your chances of quitting smoking.

Nicotine nasal spray

The nasal spray delivers a fine spray of nicotine to the nasal mucosa. It is very **quickly absorbed** and provides peak plasma concentrations in approximately ten minutes. With this rapid onset of action the nasal spray is **particularly helpful** for **highly dependent** smokers and those who want quick relief of withdrawal symptoms. However, smokers may be deterred from using this because of its initial adverse effects, such as sneezing and a burning sensation in the nose. Smokers need to be warned about these unpleasant effects, but also reassured that it does not cause any damage to their nose, and that they will get used to it after a day or two of use. The recommended dose is **one squirt** (0.5 mg) to **each nostril each hour**, with additional doses to be taken as required.

Can I get addicted to the nicotine nasal spray?

As a smoker you are already addicted to nicotine, so you will not become addicted to anything new. Furthermore, as the nicotine nasal spray provides less nicotine and more slowly than your cigarettes, the chances of you using it past three months are low. A small percentage of users do go on to use the nasal spray long-term, but these are generally smokers that need to use it for longer to stop them going back to smoking. There are no known risks of using the nasal spray long-term and in any case it is much safer than smoking.

Oral products

Nicotine absorption from the oral NRT products, including the inhalator, is via the **buccal mucosa** (the lining of the inside of the cheeks and lips). Peak plasma concentration is reached in some 20–30 minutes. These products should be **used on a regular basis** to maintain blood nicotine levels, to have the best effect; however, additional use can be helpful at times when urges to smoke are more intense or more frequent.

An initial unpleasant taste is common to all these products, and this can be a barrier to correct use. Smokers should be **reassured** that they will become tolerant of this after a short period of time (usually a couple of days). Incorrect use of oral products, for example chewing the gum too vigorously, usually results in more nicotine being swallowed. This is not hazardous but means less nicotine is absorbed, and it may cause local irritation and hiccups. Two oral nicotine products (gum and inhalator) have been licensed for **cutting down first**, and then **stopping smoking** completely, later on. Box 4.6 describes this process in more detail.

Box 4.6 Cut down then stop (CDTS) with NRT.

At the time of writing, two products (Nicorette gum and Nicorette inhalator) have been approved for use by smokers to cut down on their smoking prior to attempting to stop. There is every reason to believe that other NRT products will have similar indications approved in the future.

Smokers who are **not ready** to make a quit attempt should consider using **NRT** to help them **cut down, with a view to stopping later**. Health care professionals should advise clients to stop smoking completely, and recommend attending NHS Stop Smoking Services to help with this. However, once it is clear that a smoker is not ready to stop they should recommend NRT-assisted reduction with a view to stopping later.

The process that has been licensed for the gum and inhalator is:

Step 1	0–6 weeks	Cut down to 50% of cigarette consumption
Step 2	6 weeks–6 months	Continue to cut down, stop completely
Step 3	6–9 months	Stop smoking completely, continue NRT
Step 4	within 12 months	Stop using NRT by 12 months

See: ASH (2005) Cut Down Then Stop (CDTS): guidance for health professionals on this new indication for nicotine replacement therapy. ASH, London. **http://www.ash.org.uk/html/cessationdetail.php#reduction**

Nicotine chewing gum

Nicotine gum comes in two strengths, **2 mg and 4 mg**; more **dependent smokers** should use the **4 mg gum**. The bioavailability is not 100%; in fact the 2 mg gum typically yields only about 0.9 mg of nicotine while the 4 mg gum yields about 1.2 mg. Other oral products are similar in their nicotine delivery. Users should aim to use between 10 and 15 pieces per day. Instructing smokers to **use one piece an hour** is a convenient way to encourage the correct dosage. There is a specific technique to using the gum. Each piece should be chewed slowly in order to release the nicotine; this will be experienced as a hot peppery taste. The gum should then be 'parked' between the cheek and gums so that the nicotine can be absorbed. After a few minutes the gum can be chewed again, and then parked. This should be repeated for 20–30 minutes.

Why do I have to store this gum against my cheek? Why can't I just chew it like normal gum?

It is important to use the chew-park-chew technique with the gum. This is because the nicotine from the gum is absorbed through the lining of your mouth, so holding it against the inside of your cheek will ensure that nicotine is absorbed. If you chewed it like normal gum then much of the nicotine would be swallowed and wasted.

Nicotine sublingual tablets

These small **2 mg tablets** are made to dissolve under the tongue, although the nicotine is absorbed through any part of the oral mucosa. **Hourly use** should be recommended to achieve the best effect, but of course it can be used more frequently, or with two at a time, if desired. After 20 minutes the residual tablet can be removed.

Nicotine inhalator

The inhalator consists of a small plastic tube containing a replaceable nicotine cartridge. It may provide more behavioural replacement than the other products, but there is no strong evidence for this. Despite its name the nicotine from this device is **not inhaled into the lungs**, but deposited on the oral mucosa through which it is absorbed. To achieve sufficient blood nicotine levels the user should 'puff' on the inhalator for **20 minutes each hour**. After three 20-minute puffing sessions the cartridge should be changed. The average smoker should aim to use six cartridges per day. In cold weather it is advisable to keep the inhalator warm so that the nicotine vapour can be released from the cartridge.

Nicotine lozenge

The lozenge comes in different strengths: 1 mg (Novartis) or 2 mg (GSK) for **less dependent smokers** and 2 mg (Novartis) or 4 mg (GSK) for **more dependent smokers**. The lozenge should be dissolved in the mouth, moving it around intermittently. It can be removed after 30 minutes of use. To achieve the greatest benefit lozenges should be used regularly at the rate of approximately **one lozenge per hour** (or 15 lozenges a day).

Box 4.7 Past experiences with NRT.

There is a good chance that smokers may have tried NRT in the past and some will have found it unhelpful. When using these products without advice smokers may have had unrealistic expectations about how NRT works, may not have liked the initial taste and may not have used it correctly, or for long enough. Providing **information** on **correct usage** will help mitigate these problems. Smokers can be reassured that even if they have used NRT before and failed this is not an obstacle to future success (Shiffman et al., 2004).

How long should I use NRT for?

It is recommended that you use NRT for 8–12 weeks. Don't stop using it too soon as you will risk going back to smoking.

Box 4.8 Combining nicotine products.

Combining two NRT products to gain better control of withdrawal symptoms is a logical approach. An example would be to use a patch to provide a steady delivery of nicotine, combined with nicotine gum, to provide relief of breakthrough urges. However, some current product licensing still warns that NRT products should not be used together. This not only acts as a barrier for combination use, but also contributes to fear of medicinal nicotine among smokers and health care professionals. The **current evidence** suggests that combination treatment can provide a **small**, but significant **increase in abstinence rates** compared to a single product (OR = 1.42; 95% CI: 1.14–1.76) and, above all else, is safe (NICE, 2002; Silagy et al., 2004).

Box 4.9 Long-term NRT use.

NRT is generally used for **up to three months**. Most users will not require it for longer than this; however, a small number do. It has been reported that among those who quit using nicotine gum that they have bought, 3% continue to use it for 12 months or more (Shiffman et al., 2003). Furthermore, it seems to be the more **dependent smokers** that **use it for longer** (West et al., 2000), and if NRT is stopped too soon these smokers might relapse back to smoking. There are no real safety concerns of long-term use.

4.3.2 Bupropion

Bupropion (Zyban) is currently the only **non-nicotine** pharmacotherapy licensed for smoking cessation. It has a number of actions that are thought to contribute to its ability to help smokers quit. These include inhibition of neuronal re-uptake of dopamine and noradrenaline, non-competitive inhibition of the nicotinic acetylecholine receptor and effects on serotonin re-uptake (Richmond & Zwar, 2003). From a clinical perspective, it **helps smokers** by **reducing** the severity of withdrawal symptoms, including **the desire** or **urge to smoke**, thereby making the quit attempt easier and success more likely.

Combining the results of over twenty studies shows that compared to placebo, **bupropion** approximately **doubles the chances** of remaining abstinent for a year (Hughes et al., 2004). Currently, there is not enough evidence to suggest that combining bupropion with NRT is better than using bupropion alone.

Bupropion is a **safe medication** when prescribed appropriately (see Box 4.10). It is only available on prescription, and therefore smokers who wish to use this will need to see their GP. However, all health care professionals providing treatment for smokers should be familiar with the contraindications and cautions for using this drug (see Box 4.11).

Box 4.10 Bupropion is a safe and effective medication.

In 2001 several scare stories appeared in the UK media, suggesting that bupropion was associated with a number of deaths. However, on analysis of the post-marketing surveillance data the Committee for the Safety of Medicines stated that bupropion was not implicated as a cause of these deaths (CSM & MCA, 2001). In fact many fatalities were a consequence of a smoking-related disease.

The smoker needs to **start bupropion** approximately a **week before quitting**, allowing time for a steady state concentration to be reached. During this time they smoke as normal. Although the prescriber may discuss dosage and side effects, it is good practice to reinforce these to the smoker. Bupropion has some **common side effects** that include **dry mouth** and **insomnia**. A rash may also present. In common with other antidepressants there is a **rare risk of seizure** (reported to be less than 1 in 1000).

How do I use Zyban?

You start bupropion (Zyban) 8–14 days before you stop smoking. You take one tablet daily, in the morning, for the first six days and then increase the dose to one tablet twice daily, keeping at least eight hours between each dose. You should complete the whole course of 120 tablets, which will take about nine weeks.

Box 4.11 Bupropion (Zyban) prescribing information.

Tablets: 150 mg sustained release tablets

Dosage: start with one tablet once a day for the first six days, increasing to one tablet twice daily from day seven onwards. It is recommended to keep at least eight hours between each dose.

Treatment period: nine weeks (120 tablets)

Contraindications: allergy to bupropion; current or previous seizure disorder; brain tumour; current or previous diagnosis of bulimia or anorexia nervosa; severe hepatic cirrhosis; concomitant use of bupropion and monoamine oxidase inhibitors; history of bipolar disorder; withdrawal from alcohol or benzodiazepines; pregnancy; aged under 18.

Risk factors: a risk/benefit assessment should be undertaken before prescribing bupropion to clients with other risk factors for seizures. Factors that increase the risk of seizures include medications that lower seizure threshold (for example antidepressants, antipsychotics, antimalarials, quinolones, sedating antihistamines, systemic corticosteroids, theophylline, tramadol); alcohol abuse; history of head trauma; diabetes (see note below); and use of stimulants and anorectics.

Side effects: **common** – dry mouth, sleeping difficulties and headache. **Rare** (1 in 1000) – seizures

Special groups: **elderly** – 150 mg once daily is recommended. **Diabetes**, if diet controlled prescribe full dose. If well controlled with insulin or oral hypoglycaemics prescribe 150 mg once daily. If poorly controlled recommend NRT.

See also Appendix 1 and 2.

CSM & MCA, 2001; GlaxoSmithKline, 2001; NICE, 2002

Why do I continue to smoke during the first week of taking Zyban?

It takes at least a week for bupropion to reach a level in your blood at which it will be most effective. Therefore, you need to start taking Zyban before you stop smoking. During this time you should smoke as normal.

Support and advice

4.3.3 Explanation of medications

Medications that are available to smokers to help them in their quit attempt need to be explained to clients in an accurate and positive way that assists them in choosing which medication to use. The statement box below shows an example of explaining the **role medications have in a quit attempt.**

There are two types of medication available to help you in your quit attempt: nicotine replacement therapy (NRT), such as nicotine gum and nicotine patch, and bupropion (Zyban). Both are effective and, if used properly, will double your chances of stopping smoking – however, they are not a magic cure.

Medications are an important part of a successful quit attempt, but they are not the only part. Receiving professional support and advice from someone like me will also roughly double your chances of stopping smoking, but you will need support from other people too. You will also have to make changes to your daily routine and will have to be highly committed to give yourself a good chance of stopping smoking for good.

The statement box in Chapter 3 (Section 3.5.2.1 Nicotine replacement therapy) gives an example of how to explain the role that NRT has in a quit attempt. The following box illustrates a way of alleviating the common concerns of clients that NRT is harmful or that they will become 'addicted to nicotine'. For information on the use of NRT by adolescent smokers, those with cardiovascular disease and by pregnant or breastfeeding women see Section 4.3.5 Treatment points in special populations of smokers. An example of explaining the **safety of NRT** is shown in the statement box below.

Nicotine doesn't cause cancer; it is the tar and carbon monoxide in cigarette smoke that are harmful. NRT will not give you any of the tar and carbon monoxide that you get from cigarettes, but will give you some nicotine to reduce the withdrawal symptoms that many smokers experience when they stop smoking.

The nicotine that you do get from NRT is less than you would get from cigarettes and is absorbed more slowly in the body. This means that very few people use NRT long term, and those that do normally need it. The biggest problem with NRT use is not that people become dependent on the products, but that people do not use enough of it for long enough.

As there is no real difference in terms of effectiveness between types of NRT, the product that smokers use during their quit attempt is largely a matter of personal choice. Table 4.3 overleaf provides some basic information on the different NRT products that may help clients to make their choice and how to **use the NRT properly**. Side effects from using NRT are **minor** and, if the product continues to be used, clients will normally **get used to them after 48 hours**.

The statement box in Chapter 3 (Section 3.5.2.2 Bupropion (Zyban)) gives an example of explaining the role that **bupropion** has in a quit attempt. The following box illustrates a way of explaining that bupropion is **not suitable for all smokers**.

Zyban is an effective medication for helping people to stop smoking. However, because it has certain side effects it is not suitable for all smokers and there are a number of questions that need to be asked to make sure that it is suitable for you. Should this not be the case then there is no need to worry as NRT will be available for use by you and that is equally as effective as Zyban. ”

It is worth emphasising that bupropion is a relatively **safe medicine** and is similar to many other antidepressants. However, there are **some smokers** for whom it is **contraindicated** or **cautioned** (see Appendix 1). There are also some other **medicines** that it **interacts** with and smokers taking these medications should **not be prescribed bupropion**, or should only be done so under **caution** or **extreme caution** (see Appendix 2). Given that NRT is an equally effective alternative it seems sensible under such circumstances to **recommend the use of NRT**.

The smoker's **GP** is usually **best placed** to assess whether **bupropion is suitable** for use by them because of the contraindications and cautions associated with it, and because they have access to the client's medical notes and history. However, the checklist in Figure 4.5 may be useful for helping the smoker decide whether it is NRT or bupropion they are going to use in their quit attempt; and to avoid sending smokers for whom Zyban is not suitable to their GPs.

4.3.4 Supplying medications

Most local NHS Stop Smoking Services have mechanisms for supplying medications to clients. These may involve **voucher schemes**,

Table 4.3 Instructions for use of NRT products.

Preparation	Method of use	Initial side effects	Recommended daily dose
Transdermal patches	Place patch anywhere between neck and ankles, a relatively hairless part of the body with some fat (like the thigh or upper arm) is usually recommended. Rotate site at which patches are situated. 16-hour patch: put one patch on first thing in the morning and remove before bed. 24-hour patch: put one patch on first thing in the morning and replace with a new one the next morning. *Note: not recommended for smokers with a plaster allergy, or who suffer from eczema or psoriasis.*	Some local irritation of the skin may occur	1 patch
Sublingual tablets	Place 'microtab' under tongue and allow to dissolve. Tablet can be removed if not dissolved after 20 minutes.	Some local irritation (burning sensation) in mouth	15–20 tablets regularly throughout the day
Lozenges	Place lozenge in mouth and suck as with a sweet. Occasionally switch side of mouth lozenge is resting in, if 'held' rather than sucked. Tablet can be removed if not dissolved after 20 minutes.	Some local irritation (burning sensation) in mouth	10–15 lozenges regularly throughout the day
Chewing gum	Chew gum for a few minutes until nicotine is released – indicated by a hot peppery taste. 'Park' gum in side of mouth and let the nicotine be absorbed for a few minutes. Repeat chewing and 'park' gum in other side of mouth. Use each piece of gum for about 20 minutes. Do not chew as normal gum as this will result in less nicotine being absorbed and in a sore throat and gastric irritation. *Note: probably not recommended for smokers with dentures or who have trouble chewing.*	Some local irritation (burning sensation) in mouth. Aching jaw.	10–15 pieces regularly throughout the day
Nasal spray	Insert the nasal spray tip into the nostril, pointing the top towards the back of the nose, and squirt one shot into each nostril. *Note: probably not recommended for smokers who suffer from nasal problems.*	Some local irritation (burning sensation) in nostrils. Sneezing and eyes may water.	2 squirts regularly throughout the day.
Inhalator	After the cartridge is placed inside the inhalator and pierced, 'puff' on it as with a cigarette. The nicotine vapour is absorbed through the lining of the mouth. Use for about 20 minutes and replace cartridge after three occasions or when there is no taste to the vapour.		3–6 cartridges

Manufacturer's recommendations for use of oral products differ. The accepted wisdom is that oral products should be used hourly ('on the hour, every hour') throughout the day.

Figure 4.5 Suitability for medication.

(Place a X by any conditions that apply)	X
ZYBAN IS NOT APPROPRIATE IN ANY OF THE FOLLOWING CASES:	
(1) Clients under 18 years of age	
(2) Clients who are pregnant or breastfeeding or considering becoming pregnant	
(3) Clients with a history of epilepsy or any seizure disorder	
(4) Clients with a history of eating disorder (e.g. anorexia)	
(5) Clients with a severe liver disorder	
(6) Clients with a history of bipolar affective disorder (manic depression)	
(7) Clients with a known sensitivity to bupropion	
(8) Clients using monoamine oxidase inhibitors (MAOIs)	
ZYBAN – EXTREME CAUTION SHOULD BE EXERCISED IN ANY OF THE FOLLOWING CASES:	
(1) Clients with a history of head trauma	
(2) Clients with a brain tumour	
(3) Clients using drugs that lower the seizure threshold (e.g. antipsychotics, antidepressants, theophylline, systemic steroids, chloroquine)	
ZYBAN – CAUTION SHOULD BE EXERCISED IN ANY OF THE FOLLOWING CASES:	
(1) Clients with alcohol abuse	
(2) Clients with withdrawal from tranquilliser use	
(3) Clients with diabetes	
(4) Clients with psychosis or severe mental illness	
(5) Clients using stimulants or anorectic products	
(6) Clients using levodopa	
(7) Elderly clients (the dose should generally be 150 mg per day)	
(8) Clients with liver or kidney dysfunction (the dose should generally be 150 mg per day)	
(9) Clients who use any medication which may interact with Zyban	
(10) Clients who use any other medication	
NRT – A RISK BENEFIT ASSESSMENT SHOULD BE UNDERTAKEN IN BOTH OF THE FOLLOWING CASES (and the client's doctor informed of the decision to use NRT):	
(1) Clients who are pregnant or breastfeeding or considering becoming pregnant	
(2) Clients who have suffered an acute cardiac event or stroke in the past four weeks, or suffer with unstable angina	
Note: stopping smoking causes an alteration in the rate of metabolism of some drugs (see Appendix 3); the client's GP should be informed of this possibility so a decision can be made about altering dosages. (This is not an effect of nicotine, but of stopping smoking – components of tobacco smoke are known to increase the hepatic metabolism of various drugs.)	

Support and advice

patient group directions (PGD), or rely upon **prescriptions from GPs**. All **NRT** products are also available '**over the counter**' (OTC) at pharmacies and some (the nicotine patch and gum) are available on general sale. One week's supply of NRT usually costs £15–20. The availability of NRT products is shown in Table 4.4.

It is recommended that **supplies of NRT** be given for the following durations: two weeks, two weeks, four weeks and four weeks (12 weeks in total) (see Section 4.3.1 for information on longer-term use of NRT). NRT is usually supplied on an '**abstinence contingent**' basis to avoid wastage. In other words, clients are only given a further supply if their continued abstinence is confirmed (usually by self-report and CO validation) (see Section 4.2.4 above), or if the

Table 4.4 Availability of NRT products.

Preparation	Products	Week's supply	Availability
Transdermal patches	Nicorette 16-hour (5 mg, 10 mg and 15 mg) Nicotinell 24-hour (7 mg, 14 mg and 21 mg) NiQuitin CQ 24-hour (7 mg, 14 mg and 21 mg)	7	■ Prescription ■ Over the counter (OTC) from pharmacists ■ General sale from supermarkets
Sublingual tablets	Nicorette 2 mg	105	■ Prescription ■ Over the counter (OTC) from pharmacists
Lozenges	NicQuitin CQ 2 mg and 4 mg Nicotinell 1 mg and 2 mg *Mint flavours available*	96	■ Prescription ■ Over the counter (OTC) from pharmacists
Chewing gum	Nicorette 2 mg and 4 mg Nicotinell 2 mg and 4 mg *Mint, liquorice and fruit flavours available*	96	■ Prescription ■ Over the counter (OTC) from pharmacists ■ General sale from supermarkets
Nasal spray	Nicorette 10 ml	1 bottle	■ Prescription ■ Over the counter (OTC) from pharmacists
Inhalator	Nicorette 10 mg	42 cartridges	■ Prescription ■ Over the counter (OTC) from pharmacists

clinician thinks there is a reasonable chance that abstinence will be achieved. **Bupropion** is a prescription only medicine and should be supplied for **eight weeks** in two periods of four weeks each. A template PGD is available for NRT (including products in combination) and for bupropion on the PharmacyHealthLink website: **www.pharmacyhealthlink.org.uk**

Examples of letters that can be sent to GPs requesting that clients be considered for various medications can be viewed and downloaded from the website of the Smoking Cessation Service Research Network (SCSRN): **www.scsrn.org**

4.3.5 Treatment points in special populations of smokers

Product licences contain a number of warnings for use contributing to the reluctance of some smokers to use NRT and of some health care professionals to recommend it. Although **nicotine** is not completely without risk it **is undoubtedly safer than continued smoking.** Despite this there still seems to be a tendency to overestimate the risks of medicinal nicotine while underestimating the risks of smoking. Box 4.12 discusses some of the points to consider with adolescent smokers.

Box 4.12 Adolescent smokers.

Many young smokers show signs of nicotine dependence (McNeill, 1991). Although there is little published data demonstrating the efficacy of NRT in young smokers, there is no logical reason as to why it should not help as long as it is used correctly and the smoker is determined to give up. A number of NRT products are now licensed for use, on medical advice, in smokers under the age of 18. Ultimately the **decision to use NRT** should be based upon the smoker's **determination to quit**, and **level of dependence** as opposed to age. Given that NRT is less harmful than smoking, safety concerns should not be a barrier to use.

There are special challenges in treating young smokers and they are best directed, and assisted, towards your local Stop Smoking Service.

In its guidance document NICE made it clear that when considering the use of NRT in smokers with certain conditions (including smokers who are pregnant or breastfeeding and those with cardiovascular disease) the health care professional should **"take into account the significant harm associated with continuing to smoke and that it can be expected that NRT will deliver less nicotine (and none of the other potentially disease-causing agents) that would be obtained from cigarettes"** (NICE, 2002). Boxes 4.13 and 4.14 discuss this further.

Box 4.13 Cardiovascular disease.

Although **nicotine** has some acute effects on the cardiovascular system (CVS) it is **not a significant risk factor**, unlike tobacco smoke, for cardiovascular disease or acute cardiac events. NRT provides **less nicotine**, **less rapidly** than cigarette smoking, **without** substances like **carbon monoxide** (known to have adverse effects on the CVS). On this basis **experts agree** that all NRT products can be **safely used in smokers with stable cardiovascular disease** (McRobbie & Hajek, 2001). In smokers with **unstable disease**, or who have suffered an **acute event** in the past **four weeks** it is recommended to **assess the risks and benefits** of using NRT. If the only other option for these people is continued smoking, a risk benefit assessment invariably leads to recommending NRT. When using NRT in this group it is advisable to use the **shorter acting oral products** that can be discontinued immediately in the event of any problems. Nicotine patches, even once removed, leave a small reservoir of nicotine under the skin.

I had a heart attack last year; can I use the nasal spray?

It is safe for you to use the nasal spray. Nicotine does not cause heart disease; it is the other constituents of cigarette smoke (for example carbon monoxide) that cause the damage.

Box 4.14 Pregnant and breastfeeding women.

Smoking during pregnancy is associated with **large risks** to both the **mother** and **fetus**, and later to the newborn and growing infant. Although nicotine itself may be implicated in some of the adverse effects of smoking (for example behavioural problems in the infant and low birth-weight), it is worth remembering that NRT delivers much less nicotine than cigarettes and without the other harmful ingredients of tobacco smoke. Clearly, it is better for pregnant women to be both nicotine and tobacco free. However, for many this is extremely difficult and NRT in combination with structured support and advice may be needed to help achieve abstinence. Product licences are changing slowly, and some now suggest that **NRT use may be considered** in pregnant women who are **unable to give up without** the use of NRT. When considering NRT use it is prudent to document discussion of risks and benefits, and **initially oral products** should be **recommended**, as these will provide less nicotine to the fetus than a patch. However, if oral products are not tolerated then a 16-hour patch may be recommended, but this must be removed before going to bed. Treatment should be provided as early in the pregnancy as possible, with the aim to be smoke free and nicotine free by the third trimester.

NRT use whilst breastfeeding is associated with very few risks. Nicotine does accumulate in breast milk; however, relatively little is absorbed from the infant's gut. The risks associated with environmental tobacco smoke are much greater than any risk that might be associated with this level of nicotine.

Treating pregnant smokers involves specific challenges (such as the immediacy of the need for cessation and fear by the mother of being judged), and clients may be best supported by a specialist smoking and pregnancy advisory service where these exist.

Box 4.11 and Appendix 1 give information on the prescribing of bupropion to special populations of smokers.

4.3.6 Other medications

Nortriptyline has been demonstrated to help smokers, but is not routinely used because it is not licensed. With the commercial success of NRT and Zyban, many pharmaceutical companies are examining medications that may help smokers to stop.

Varenicline is a partial nicotine agonist, meaning that it binds to and triggers the ACh (nicotinic) receptors in the brain. It has been developed from cytisine, a substance naturally occurring in the golden rain plant (*Citisus laborinum*). It has been found to be safe and effective in clinical trials and is likely to receive a licence in the near future. The main side effect is slight nausea, but no serious side effects attributable to the medication have been reported so far.

Rimonabant is a cannabinoid receptor antagonist; it binds to and blocks specific receptors in the brain involved with craving and appetite. Studies show that it has a broadly similar effectiveness to NRT but may have a greater effect in limiting weight gain. It is likely to receive a licence in the near future.

Studies are currently underway to develop a **nicotine vaccine**. Nicotine is too small to be recognised by the immune system, but when presented bound to a larger substance, antibodies can bind to nicotine, which means that it cannot pass through the blood-brain barrier and so has no effect. Licences for nicotine vaccines are probably a few years away.

Poor nicotine metabolisers smoke little and are less likely to become dependent. **Methoxsalen** has been shown to lead to smoking reduction and to increase the effects of NRT; it works by lowering the activity of the nicotine-breaking enzyme (CYP2A6). It is unlikely to be licensed for smoking cessation within the next few years.

Glucose tablets have been found to reduce the desire to smoke acutely in abstaining smokers, but there is no clear evidence that adding these to the diet improves long-term success at stopping smoking. A fuller review of these, and other, medications that may help smokers to stop can be found elsewhere (McRobbie et al., 2005).

4.4 Behavioural support – withdrawal oriented treatment

Many specialist smoking cessation services use **withdrawal oriented therapy** (Hajek, 1989). This treatment model focuses on preventing relapse in the early stages of a quit attempt by providing **intensive support** when withdrawal symptoms are at their worst, close **supervision of medication use**, and emphasising the importance of **complete abstinence**. Treatment is delivered by **specialist advisers** over six or seven sessions at weekly intervals, in groups, or one to one. Both formats are shown to **increase long-term success** compared to minimal interventions, (for example Sutherland, 2003), although data from the NHS Stop Smoking Services has shown that group treatment is associated with slightly better success rates (Bauld et al., 2003; McEwen et al., 2006).

Community advisers (typically community pharmacists, practice nurses and health visitors) deliver treatment to individuals on a part-time or sessional basis and provide an alternative to treatment at a centrally based clinic.

The following guidance offers an aide-memoire of the key steps that should be covered when providing smoking cessation treatment.

4.4.1 Preparation

The first session with the smoker is primarily about explaining what the treatment entails, and maximising their commitment to and **preparing** for, their target quit date. It will encompass the initial assessment, including the explanation of **CO testing**, discussion of **past quit** attempts, **guidance** on what **medication** to use, how to get the most out of it and, if appropriate, how to get a prescription from their GP. This session will also involve providing **accurate information** about **what to expect** during the quit attempt and how to **deal with difficult situations**. The preparation appointment will probably last 30–45 minutes and will usually take place one or two weeks before the quit date. An outline of this appointment is given in Box 4.15.

Shouldn't I cut down the number of cigarettes that I'm smoking in the week leading up to my quit date?

The problem with this approach is that by smoking less cigarettes each one may become that little bit more important to you. Psychologically this probably doesn't help when it comes to your quit date, and you will not be any better off physically as you will smoke each cigarette more intensively. So, as this is your last week of smoking, you might as well smoke as normal and begin preparing yourself for your quit date.

Box 4.15 The preparation appointment.

(1) **Explain the treatment you offer:**
- evidence-based treatment combining support/advice and medication
- five further sessions on a weekly basis

(2) **Make sure your client is motivated to quit at this time:**
- explain that even with the help available, substantial determination and effort may be required, and ask: "Are you ready to make a serious attempt to stop smoking?"
- check that they can attend all the treatment sessions
- advise that if they are not 100% sure at this time they can come back and see you at any time in the future

(3) **Set a quit date:**
- explain the importance of choosing a day to quit smoking (typically the day of next week's session)
- arrange an appropriate date to quit
- advise to smoke as normal up until the quit date
- advise that cutting down doesn't work (see Section 3.3.2)
- explain that the goal from the quit date onwards is **not to have a single puff**

(4) **Explain the withdrawal syndrome:**
- explain that many smokers experience a range of different symptoms when they stop (see Section 3.4.3)
- reassure that most symptoms last 2–4 weeks and will get less severe and less frequent the longer they go without a single puff
- explain that medication (NRT or bupropion) will help reduce the severity of withdrawal discomfort

(5) **Assess the level of tobacco dependence** (see Section 4.2.1)

(6) **Measure carbon monoxide level in expired breath:**
- explain that this is one of the many harmful elements of cigarettes
- explain that it gives an indication of their cigarette use
- use the CO reading to provide motivation (that is, this will drop within a week of the client stopping smoking); explain that you will repeat the test at every session

(7) **Discuss medications and arrange a supply:**
- explain the two different types of medication available and how they work (see Sections 3.5.2 and 4.3.3)
- if **bupropion** is the product of choice they need to start this a week before quitting (see Section 4.3.2)
- if **NRT** is the product of choice then discuss the six different types, and offer some advice on what product might be most suitable (see Section 4.3.1); explain that they will start their NRT on the quit date and you will show them how to use it, so they have to bring their first box of NRT along with them
- arrange for a supply of medication (see Section 4.3.4)

(8) **Advise on preparing to stop:**
- suggest that by the quit date all cigarettes, lighters and ashtrays are cleared out of the house, car, office, etc.
- ask them to consider which cigarettes are going to be missed most and how they might be able to deal with this
- advise on strategies of how to cope with urges to smoke (see Section 4.4.3)
- suggest that they tell all their friends, family and colleagues (especially those that smoke) about their quit attempt and ask for their support

4.4.2 Quit date

The client's **last cigarette** should be smoked **immediately prior to** this quit date appointment. This session with the smoker will ensure that they have a sufficient **supply of medication**, and will reinforce instructions on **dosage** and **usage**. This session will also involve boosting motivation, reinforcing the '**not-even-one-puff**' message and planning for the week ahead. The quit day appointment will probably last 15–20 minutes. (See Box 4.16.)

Box 4.16 Quit day.

(1) **Ask how client feels about quitting:**
- provide reassurance if worried, and reinforce the benefits of quitting
- ensure that client has discarded all cigarettes

(2) **Measure carbon monoxide in expired breath**

(3) **Discuss medication issues:**

Bupropion
- check usage and answer any questions
- summarise again how it will help (reducing withdrawal, increases success)
- enquire about any side effects

NRT
- provide the rationale for using NRT (reduces withdrawal, increases success)

- ask client to start using NRT and advise on correct use and dosage
- reassure about initial unpleasant effects (will get used to the taste), and any safety concerns (NRT does not cause cancer, provides less nicotine than cigarettes)

(4) **Explain the importance of complete abstinence:**
- reinforce that having just a puff will put them right back to the beginning, stopping completely will make it easier and they will get through the withdrawal phase faster

(5) **Advise on coping:**
- suggest techniques such as distraction, avoiding difficult situations, exercise, and using medication (see Section 4.4.3 below)
- suggest where the client can get additional support (see Appendix 4)

(6) **Summarise:**
- not a single puff
- take it step by step
- it will get easier over time
- importance of making a good start

Is it better to stop smoking when I'm ready, or to set a quit date and stick to that?

It is better to set a quit date and stick to it. This will help you prepare for quitting and will give you something to aim for. You will be able to make sure that you have got rid of all your cigarettes by this date and that you have a supply of medication to use from then on. I can guide you through this process and help you set a quit date so that you feel ready.

Support and advice

4.4.3 Urges to smoke and what to do about them

When smokers get a strong urge for a cigarette they normally smoke and the feeling goes away temporarily. This is not an option when stopping smoking as the **only way for the urges to reduce is not to smoke at all**.

At first, the urge to smoke can feel overwhelming, especially if it takes clients by surprise. In the first few days and weeks **these urges can be very strong** and can occur a lot. **Urges do pass and can be controlled**. As long as clients do not smoke after their quit date then over the next few weeks **they will get less strong and less frequent**, and they will get better at dealing with them.

There will be all sorts of things that will be linked with smoking in a client's mind. The following list shows the more common **triggers**:

- Stress
- Arguments
- Other people smoking
- Alcohol
- Passing places where cigarettes are normally bought
- Cups of coffee and tea
- Seeing cigarettes lying around
- The smell of tobacco smoke
- New social situations
- Anxiety
- Boredom
- Favourite smoking places
- Activities where smoking is common
- Memories
- After meals

Each time a client copes with a triggered urge to smoke it may get a little easier next time, but they **should not** get complacent or **test themselves** by unnecessary exposure to smokers or **high-risk situations**. They will change from day to day and a situation they coped with easily one day may be more of a challenge the next. **In time they will find the triggers lose their strength, but it is best to allow this to happen naturally.** The most common treatments for tobacco withdrawal symptoms are nicotine replacement and bupropion (Zyban). There is no clear evidence yet that one form of nicotine replacement is more effective at treating withdrawal than others, though more rapid delivery systems (for example nasal spray) give more rapid acute relief. Boxes 4.17 and 4.18 show strategies that may be used.

What should I do when I have a really strong temptation to smoke?

Everyone deals with temptations to smoke in different ways. The most important thing to remember is that these urges pass after a short time, and the longer you go without a single puff on a cigarette the less frequent they will become. There are a number of strategies that people have found to be helpful for dealing with these temptations including distracting yourself by keeping busy, avoiding situations where you know you might be tempted to smoke, exercising and, of course, using your medication which is proven to help.

Box 4.17 Strategies for dealing with urges to smoke.

Nicotine replacement therapy (NRT): the products should be used regularly as described in Section 4.3.1. Most NRT products take a while to raise nicotine levels in the body and so it is no good clients waiting until they get an urge before using them.

Glucose: there is good evidence that glucose (glucose tablets from your pharmacist) will reduce urges when they arise. Clients should check with their doctor if they are diabetic.

Exercise: short (five-minute) bursts of 'moderate' intensity exercise (such as walking briskly or walking up flights of stairs) also appear to reduce urges. Clients should check with their doctor if they have not done any exercise for a while.

Distraction: at times clients may just have to 'grit their teeth' and get through the urges, but keeping busy and doing something active may help focus their attention on something other than the urge to smoke.

Avoidance: if there are certain situations (such as the pub, the coffee break, or socialising with smokers) in which clients experience more urges, or more severe urges, then they should try and avoid them in the first few weeks.

Box 4.18 Increased appetite and what to do about it.

Increased appetite is one of the tobacco withdrawal symptoms and can go on for some time. For most people this signals weight gain, although the **main reason** for **weight gain** is a **drop in metabolic rate** after the quit date. Although concern over weight gain prevents some smokers from making an attempt to stop smoking, the **putting on of weight is not a major factor in people abandoning their quit attempt**.

Most people put on an average of between 3–8 kg (7–18 lbs), although of course this need not be the case if clients eat less or exercise more. The problem is, as most experts agree, that one major health behaviour change (that is, stopping smoking) is enough at any one time. **Trying to stop smoking, changing diet and increasing the amount of physical activity may result in clients failing in all three.** The best course of action appears to be to concentrate on stopping smoking, as this is the one thing that is going to have the biggest impact on health. Then, if the client has managed not to smoke at all for a couple of months, and they are feeling more confident that they are an ex-smoker, they can look at changing their diet and exercising more.

Support and advice

4.4.4 Post-quit sessions

The first three weekly appointments after the quit day normally follow the same pattern: **review the previous week**, **check on medication** usage and supply, **plan for the coming week** and **boost motivation**. This session may only last 10–15 minutes if the client is doing well, although those who struggle may require somewhat longer sessions. Box 4.19 outlines the format of sessions.

Box 4.19 At each week after the quit date.

(1) **Discuss how the week went:**
If abstinent
- congratulate and give praise
- reinforce the importance of not a single puff

If had a few 'slips'
- acknowledge the effort made, but reinforce the rationale of complete abstinence
- each slip puts them back to the quit date
- having the odd cigarette makes the withdrawal worse
- they will find it much easier to stop smoking altogether

If cut down
- acknowledge that cutting down might seem a good idea, but explain why it doesn't work (see Section 3.3.2)
- if the client is smoking daily, suggest setting a new quit date and reinforce the rationale of complete abstinence

(2) **Check for withdrawal discomfort:**
- reassure that most of the withdrawal symptoms are short-lived (see Section 3.4.3)

(3) **Measure carbon monoxide:**
- to confirm abstinence and to boost motivation

(4) **Check on medication use:**
- reassure that they will get used to the unpleasant taste/sensation
- enquire about any side effects
- check dosage, supply and any problems with use; look out for insufficient use of oral NRT

(5) **Discuss coming week:**
- identify times when client feels they may be at risk and discuss ways of coping

(6) **Summarise:**
- not a single puff
- take it step by step
- it will get easier over time

Now that I have not smoked for a few weeks, should I start to come off the medication?

You are doing well to have quit for this time. However, it is still 'early days' and the medication has definitely been helping you not to smoke. I would advise you to continue with your medication for the recommended 8–12 weeks. Remember that this medication is perfectly safe and you should be able to stop using it without any problem when it is time. Stopping too soon could jeopardise your efforts so far.

4.4.5 End of treatment and relapse prevention

At the end of treatment it is important to ensure that the client has a sufficient supply of their medication and is aware of where they can get **ongoing support**. There is **limited evidence** for any effective **relapse prevention interventions**. However, clients should be aware of **high risk situations** and there are a number of basic strategies that can be communicated. For example, clients can be made aware that although sometimes ex-smokers get over an isolated lapse, in the great majority of cases this leads to a full relapse. Before having a single puff they should ask themselves whether they want to go back to smoking. If the answer is 'No' then they should not have a puff. This session usually lasts 20–30 minutes.

In quit attempts where the client is unable to stop smoking there remains an opportunity to 'debrief' them, so that they are not deterred from making another quit attempt and from getting help from NHS Stop Smoking Services in the future. The statement box below gives an example of debriefing a client who has been **unsuccessful in their quit attempt**.

As you know, stopping smoking can be difficult and many smokers need more than one attempt to stop smoking for good. Just because you did not make it this time it does not mean that you will not be successful in the future, and this experience should not deter you from trying again. Hopefully, you might have learnt something from this attempt which will put you in a better position next time. The best thing that you can do now is take a break, 'recharge your batteries', and in a few months time think about preparing to make another attempt at stopping smoking.

Box 4.20 End of treatment.

(1) **Medication use:**
- advise bupropion users to complete the course of 120 tablets (~9 weeks)
- advise NRT users that they should continue for up to 12 weeks
- oral NRT or nasal spray can still be used opportunistically

(2) **Discuss potential relapse situations** (see Section 4.1.4)

(3) **Advise on coping with potential relapse situations:**
- advise on boosting motivation to maintain abstinence
- oral NRT or nasal spray can still be used opportunistically

(4) **Discuss any ongoing support:**
- returning for continued supply of NRT
- local Stop Smoking Services may offer ongoing support
- suggest where they can get additional support (see Appendix 4)

Box 4.21 Personal issues and counselling.

> Behavioural support for smoking cessation is a very focused treatment. Occasionally, there are clients who may have needs and personal issues that extend beyond this. If you think that these clients require professional input then refer/direct them to appropriate services and try and concentrate on helping them stop smoking.

4.5 Monitoring

Monitoring the quality of Stop Smoking Services should strike a balance between the need to ensure that the assessment is rigorous, objective and appropriately targeted, and the effort and resources diverted from actual service provision needed to do this.

For those working within NHS Stop Smoking Services (as full-time advisers or as community advisers) submitting figures for monitoring is part of routine practice: whether purely the minimum data set, or more comprehensive data on clients and/or a record of the stop smoking interventions they deliver.

4.5.1 National monitoring

Currently, the English Department of Health requires stop smoking services to submit quarterly 'returns' for the number of clients treated by the service. These returns are based upon a '**minimum data set**':

- Gender
- Whether pregnant (at quit date)
- Year of birth
- Ethnic group (white, mixed, asian, black, other & not known)
- Whether client has received NRT
- Whether client has received bupropion (Zyban)
- Quit date
- Whether follow-up at four weeks was completed
- Date of last cigarette

- Has client quit smoking at four-week follow-up (based on self-report)?
- Carbon monoxide validation attempted at four-week follow-up?
- If validation attempted, does carbon monoxide measurement at four-week follow-up confirm non-smoking status?

Service and monitoring guidance for NHS Smoking Cessation Services (Department of Health, 2001) can be viewed and downloaded from the website of the Smoking Cessation Service Research Network (SCSRN) (**www.scsrn.org**). Scottish services have a more extensive minimum data set which takes more account of the client characteristics (Scottish Executive, 2001).

4.5.2 Local monitoring

Many services collect **additional data** to monitor the **quality** of their service, carry out **research** and assist with **service delivery**. At the very least, this might include clients' postcodes and consent to carry out 52-week follow-ups. Other data collected might include:

- Marital status
- Whether client shares accommodation with smoker
- Highest educational achievement
- More detailed ethnicity status
- Past quit attempts
- History of medication use during past quit attempts
- Employment status
- A measure of dependence (Fagerström test for nicotine dependence (FTND))
- How client heard about the service
- Physical health
- Mental health
- Whether client smokes hand-rolled cigarettes

Examples of additional data that can collected, viewed and downloaded from the website of the Smoking Cessation Service Research Network (SCSRN): **www.scsrn.org**

Local monitoring information

Name of contact:	Address data has to be returned to:	Frequency of data returns:

4.6 Multiple choice questions

Question 1: Regarding the assessment of abstinence, which of the following statements is FALSE?

- **a** Self-reported abstinence can be obtained over the phone
- **b** Validation to confirm self-reports should be undertaken
- **c** Point prevalence abstinence rates report the percentage of clients not smoking at one point in time (e.g. over the week prior to follow-up)
- **d** Continuous abstinence rates report the percentage of clients continuously abstinent from their quit day to the follow-up point
- **e** Point prevalence gives an underestimation of the true abstinence rate

Question 2: 50 people are invited to attend a group clinic, 25 people attend the first session and 20 set a quit date. At four weeks: five have relapsed, five cannot be contacted and ten clients are validated four-week abstainers. What is the short-term quit rate for the service?

- **a** 20%
- **b** 40%
- **c** 50%
- **d** 67%
- **e** 100%

Question 3: A one-year follow-up of 100 clients that set a quit date and achieved a four-week abstinence rate of 60% reveals that: 20 are still not smoking, 10 are smoking and the remaining 30 clients are lost to follow-up. What is the one-year abstinence rate?

- **a** 67%
- **b** 50%
- **c** 33%
- **d** 30%
- **e** 20%

Question 4: What is the reported short-term abstinence rate for England and Wales Stop Smoking Services?

- **a** 23%
- **b** 32%
- **c** 53%
- **d** 62%
- **e** 74%

Question 5: What percentage of clients using the English Stop Smoking Services are expected to be one-year abstainers?

- **a** 5%
- **b** 7%
- **c** 15%
- **d** 25%
- **e** 53%

Question 6: What increases in long-term abstinence rates can a service that provides intensive behavioural support and medication be expected to achieve?

- **a** 1–3%
- **b** 6–9%
- **c** 13–19%
- **d** 21–25%
- **e** 32–37%

Question 7: Regarding relapse, which of the following statements is FALSE?

- **a** A lapse usually precedes full relapse to smoking
- **b** Going on holiday is a common reason for relapse
- **c** Use of NRT may help prevent relapse
- **d** Relapse is greatest in the first week of the quit attempt
- **e** There is good evidence for the effectiveness of cognitive behavioural therapy to prevent relapse

Question 8: Regarding the assessment of nicotine dependence, which of the following statements is FALSE?

- **a** Assessment enables the provision of appropriate treatment
- **b** Cigarette consumption is a strong indicator of dependence
- **c** A client who smokes within 30 minutes of waking is a more dependent smoker
- **d** The FTND is a six-item questionnaire that measures dependence

e Smokers can reduce their cigarette consumption, but compensate for a lesser number smoked

Question 9: Regarding the stages of change model, which of the following statements is FALSE?

a This is also known as the Transtheoretical model
b It divides smokers into different stages
c It is an essential tool for the Stop Smoking Services
d It may indicate the wrong intervention strategy
e It may lead to effective interventions not being offered to people who would have responded

Question 10: Regarding carbon monoxide (CO) and CO monitoring, which of the following statements is FALSE?

a The cut-off for being a non-smoker is 7 ppm
b CO binds to haemoglobin more strongly than oxygen
c CO reading is affected by the time of day
d CO is linked to cardiovascular disease and problems in pregnancy
e When using a CO monitor clients should hold their breath for 15 seconds

Question 11: A client who reports he is not smoking has a CO reading of 16 ppm. Which one of the following is NOT a possible explanation?

a The client is misreporting
b The client lives with a smoker
c The client has a faulty gas heater
d The client is lactose intolerant
e The client has been working with paint stripper

Question 12: Regarding NRT, which of the following statements is FALSE?

a Choice of NRT product should be determined by a health care professional
b More dependent smokers should use a higher dose or faster acting NRT product
c All NRT products are equally effective
d NRT should be considered for pregnant smokers who want to quit
e There are currently six different NRT products to choose from

Question 13: Regarding the nicotine patch, which of the following statements is FALSE?

a They are available in two different preparations
b The 24-hour patch is proven to be more effective in more dependent smokers
c Weaning patches are available, but their use is not strictly necessary

d Clients who are allergic to sticking plaster should not use the patch

e Out of all the products, patches provide the slowest delivery of nicotine

Question 14: Regarding the nicotine nasal spray, which of the following statements is FALSE?

a Nicotine is absorbed via the nasal mucosa

b Clients should be warned that it is aversive to use at first but that they will get used to it

c Nicotine from the spray can damage the nasal mucosa if used for more than three months

d Clients should be instructed to use it on a regular basis

e It can be purchased over the counter

Question 15: Regarding cutting down to stop, which of the following statements is FALSE?

a All NRT products are approved for this use

b This strategy can be considered for smokers who don't currently want to stop

c In the first six weeks clients should aim to cut down their consumption by 50%

d Clients should aim to stop smoking completely within 6–9 months

e This strategy might work by increasing the client's confidence

Question 16: Regarding oral NRT products, which of the following statements is FALSE?

a Nicotine is absorbed through the buccal mucosa

b Peak plasma concentrations are reached in 20–30 minutes

c Products are best used on a regular basis

d Clients should be instructed to use some 15 pieces of gum a day

e Swallowed nicotine lozenges can cause nicotine overdose

Question 17: Regarding long-term NRT use, which of the following statements is FALSE?

a Most clients will not need NRT past three months

b Some 20% of clients using gum will continue use for up to a year

c Dependent smokers may need to use NRT for longer than three months

d There are no real safety concerns of long-term use

e Safety concerns may deter use of NRT

Question 18: Regarding combining NRT products, which of the following statements is FALSE?

a Combination treatments are safe

b Patch and gum is a sensible combination

c Some product licences warn that combinations should not be used

d Combinations may give better withdrawal relief

e Combinations are twice as effective as using a single product

Question 19: Regarding bupropion, which of the following statements is FALSE?

a One of its cessation effects may be via its action as a non-competitive inhibitor of the nACh receptor

b It increases the neuronal re-uptake of dopamine

c It inhibits the neuronal re-uptake of noradrenaline

d It may have an effect on serotonin

e Its exact mode of action in helping smokers stop is not fully understood

Question 20: Regarding bupropion, which of the following statements is TRUE?

a It triples the chance of long-term abstinence

b It has a higher risk of seizure than other antidepressants

c It is three times more effective than NRT

d It can be used safely in combination with NRT, although evidence on the effectiveness of this is weak

e It is recommended only for smokers who have tried and failed on NRT

Question 21: Regarding bupropion dosage, which of the following statements is FALSE?

a It should be started 8–14 days prior to the quit day

b Clients smoke as normal up until their quit day

c Clients use one tablet daily for the first 8–14 days then one tablet twice daily

d A minimum of eight hours should be kept between each dose

e Dosage may need to be reduced in the elderly

Question 22: Which of the following is not a contraindication for using bupropion?

a Cardiovascular disease

b History of seizure

c History of eating disorder

d Pregnancy

e Concurrent use of monoamine oxidase inhibitors

Question 23: Which one of the following is NOT a common side effect of bupropion?

a Headache

b Dry mouth

c Insomnia

d Gastrointestinal upset

e Seizure

Question 24: Regarding withdrawal oriented treatment, which of the following statements is FALSE?

a It is an effective behavioural method for smoking cessation

b It focuses on preventing relapse in the early stages of a quit attempt

c It emphasises complete abstinence

d It is delivered by a series of lectures

e It can be used in a group or individual format

Question 25: Regarding urges to smoke, which of the following statements is FALSE?

a They last less than 48 hours

b They become less frequent over time

c They can be reduced by using NRT or bupropion

d They are often triggered by stress

e They can be alleviated by exercise

Question 26: On average, how much weight is gained in clients who stop smoking for a year?

a 0 kg

b 1–2 kg

c 3–8 kg

d 8–10 kg

e 14–16 kg

References

Abbot, N.C., Stead, L.F., White, A.R., Barnes, J. & Ernst, E. (2000). Hypnotherapy for smoking cessation. *Cochrane Database of Systematic Reviews*, *2*, CD001008.

Bauld, L., Chesterman, J., Judge, K., Pound, E. & Coleman, T. (2003). Impact of UK National Health Service smoking cessation services: variations in outcomes in England. *Tobacco Control*, *12* (3), 296–301.

Committee on Safety of Medicines and the Medicines Control Agency (2001). Zyban (bupropion (amfebutamone)), safety reminder. *Current Problems in Pharmacovigilance*, 27.

Department of Health (1998). *Smoking Kills: A White Paper on Tobacco*. London: The Stationery Office.

Department of Health (2001). *NHS Smoking Cessation Services: Service and Monitoring Guidance*. London: Department of Health.

DiClemente, C.C., Prochaska, J.O., Fairhurst, S.K., Velicer, W.F., Velasquez, M.M. & Rossi, J.S. (1991). The process of smoking cessation: an analysis of precontemplation, contemplation and preparation stages of change. *Journal of Consulting and Clinical Psychology, 59* (2), 295–304.

Ferguson, J., Bauld, L., Chesterman, J. & Judge, K. (2005). The English smoking treatment services: one-year outcomes. *Addiction, April, 100* (Suppl. 2), 59–69.

GlaxoSmithKline (2001). *Zyban (Bupropion hydrochloride) Summary of Product Characteristics*. Brentford, Middlesex GlaxoSmithKline.

Hajek, P. (1989). Withdrawal-oriented therapy for smokers. *British Journal of Addiction, 84* (6), 591–598.

Hajek, P., Stead, L.F., West, R., Jarvis, M., & Lancaster, T. (2005). Relapse prevention interventions for smoking cessation. *The Cochrane Database of Systematic Reviews*, Issue 1. Art. No.: CD003999. DOI: 10.1002/14651858.CD003999.pub2.

Health Development Agency (2002). *Standard for Training in Smoking Cessation Treatments*. London: Health Development Agency.

Heatherton, T., Kozlowski, L., Frecker, R. & Fagerström, K. (1991). The Fagerström Test for Nicotine Dependence: a revision of the Fagerström Tolerance Questionnaire. *British Journal of Addiction, 86* (9), 1119–1127.

Hughes, J.R., Stead, L.F. & Lancaster, T. (2004). Antidepressants for smoking cessation. *Cochrane Database of Systematic Reviews*, (4), CD000031.pub2.

McEwen, A., West, R. & McRobbie, H. (2006). Effectiveness of specialist group treatment for smoking cessation vs one-to-one treatment in primary care. *Addictive Behaviours*, in press.

McNeill, A.D. (1991). The development of dependence on smoking in children. *British Journal of Addiction, 86* (5), 589–592.

McRobbie, H. & Hajek, P. (2001). Nicotine replacement therapy in patients with cardiovascular disease: guidelines for health professionals. *Addiction, 96* (11), 1547–1551.

McRobbie, H., Lee, M. & Juniper, Z. (2005). Non-nicotine pharmacotherapies for smoking cessation. *Respiratory Medicine* (99), 1203–1212.

National Institute of Clinical Excellence (2002). *Guidance on the Use of Nicotine Replacement Therapy (NRT) and Bupropion for Smoking Cessation*. London: NICE.

Piasecki, T.M., Fiore, M.C., McCarthy, D.E. & Baker, T.B. (2002). Have we lost our way? The need for dynamic formulations of smoking relapse proneness. *Addiction, 97* (9), 1093–1108.

Raw, M., McNeill, A. & West, R. (1998). Smoking cessation guidelines for health professionals. A guide to effective smoking cessation interventions for the health care system. Health Education Authority. *Thorax, 53* (Suppl. 5 Pt 1), S1–19.

Richmond, R. & Zwar, N. (2003). Review of bupropion for smoking cessation. *Drug Alcohol Review, 22* (2), 203–220.

Scottish Executive (2001). *Guidance on the NHS Smoking Cessation Services in August 2001*. NHS Circular: HDL (2001) 64. Edinburgh: Scottish Executive. See 'Tobacco Unwrapped', specialist subsite of www.hebs.com

Shiffman, S., Hughes, J.R., Pillitteri, J.L. & Burton, S.L. (2003). Persistent use of nicotine replacement therapy: an analysis of actual purchase patterns in a population based sample. *Tobacco Control*, *12* (3), 310–316.

Shiffman, S., Dresler, C.M. & Rohay, J.M. (2004). Successful treatment with a nicotine lozenge of smokers with prior failure in pharmacological therapy. *Addiction*, *99* (1), 83–92.

Silagy, C., Lancaster, T., Stead, L., Mant, D. & Fowler, G. (2004). Nicotine replacement therapy for smoking cessation. *Cochrane Database of Systematic Reviews*, (3), CD000146.

Sutherland, G. (2003). Evidence for counselling effectiveness for smoking cessation. *Journal of Clinical Psychiatry Monograph*, *18* (1), 22–34.

Sutton, S. (2001). Back to the drawing board? A review of applications of the Transtheoretical model to substance use. *Addiction, Jan. 96* (1), 175–186.

West, R. (2005a). Assessing smoking cessation performance in NHS Stop Smoking Services: The Russell Standard (Clinical). Smoking Cessation Services research network (SCSRN) website: www.scsrn.org

West, R. (2005b). Time for a change: putting the Transtheoretical (Stages of change) model to rest. *Addiction, Aug. 100* (8), 1036–1039.

West, R., Hajek, P., Foulds, J., Nilsson, F., May, S. & Meadows, A. (2000). A comparison of the abuse liability and dependence potential of nicotine patch, gum, spray and inhaler. *Psychopharmacology*, *149* (3), 198–202.

West, R. & Shiffman, S. (2004). *Smoking Cessation. Fast Facts: Indispensable Guides to Clinical Practice*. Oxford: Health Press Limited.

White, A.R., Resch, K.L. & Ernst, E. (1999). A meta-analysis of acupuncture techniques for smoking cessation. *Tobacco Control*, *8* (4), 393–397.

Chapter 5

Telephone counselling

Knowledge and skills relating to telephone counselling were not included as a key learning outcome in the Health Development Agency training standard (HDA, 2002), upon which this manual is based. However, telephone counselling is included in this manual because of the role it can play in the recruitment, treatment and follow-up of clients of NHS Stop Smoking Services.

5.1 Recruiting smokers into treatment by telephone

More than **half of smokers** who use the NHS Stop Smoking Services **refer themselves**, with referrals from GPs being the next largest source (Judge et al., 2005). Smokers that refer themselves find out about local NHS Stop Smoking Services in a number of ways (for example from health professionals, referral cards, posters and local advertising), but common to all is promotion of the local service's telephone number. Although some services now offer treatment to which a smoker can 'drop-in' without an appointment (for example Adams et al., 2005; Johnstone, 2005), virtually all provide a **local telephone number** through which smokers can access **advice** and **treatment**. Some services have invested in freephone lines so that there are no financial barriers to smokers wanting to access the service.

Smokers should be able to call at any time of day. During working hours the phone line should be answered personally, wherever possible, and an answer machine should record a message at other times. As smokers' motivation to stop can change quickly, every effort should be made to contact clients as soon as possible.

Figure 5.1 provides an example of what staff can say in response to telephone calls to the service from clients.

Figure 5.1 Telephone call flow chart.

Hello, this is the smokers' support line, how can I help?

If the purpose of the call is not clear from the client's response, ask:

Are you looking for specific help to stop smoking or would you like some general information about stopping smoking?

General information

There are many written materials available for smokers thinking of quitting. These can be mailed out. This is also an opportune moment to provide some motivational support.

Stopping smoking is the best thing you can do to improve your current and future health, as well as save some money. When you are ready to stop we can help you. We offer state of the art treatment that is free and effective. Call us back on this same number whenever you are ready.

Help to stop smoking

There are two levels of support we can offer. The first is to attend a ***specialist Stop Smoking Clinic****. These clinics provide the most successful treatment. The main components of the treatment are the use of medications (e.g. NRT or bupropion) and group or individual support. The treatment programme involves attending a weekly session for 5–6 weeks, with further support available after this if you need it. You'll be quitting with a number of other smokers and it is particularly suited for dependent smokers who find quitting difficult.*

The second option is to stop with the support of a local ***community adviser*** *based in a local pharmacy or GP practice. They will also provide advice on quitting and on medication. We have a network of local advisers and can give you a phone number for the one nearest to you.*

Which option would you prefer?

Community adviser	Smokers' clinic	If still unsure
The client should be provided with details on how to arrange a session with a local community adviser. An up-to-date record of all advisers should be kept. It is practical to list these by location so that the client can choose which would be most convenient.	Client details should be taken so that they can be sent an information pack, and called back if necessary. There may also be a variety of locations and times the client can choose from.	Some further explanation might be helpful. *In general, people smoking within 30 minutes of waking up often find quitting smoking difficult and are likely to benefit from specialist help.*

The option to Cut Down Then Stop (CDTS) with NRT (see Section 4.3.1 Nicotine replacement therapy) could also be mentioned during this initial telephone contact, but each NHS Stop Smoking Service needs to develop a protocol for this.

5.2 Behavioural support by telephone

5.2.1 Telephone counselling

Telephone counselling is an **effective method** for smoking cessation, although it does not achieve such high long-term abstinence rates as face-to-face counselling (see Table 4.2).

Telephone counselling can be a cost-effective, wide-reach approach and there is some evidence that some smokers would prefer telephone over face-to-face counselling (Zhu, 2005). Telephone support can be **reactive** or **proactive**, and it is the latter technique that has the strongest evidence for efficacy. Reactive support relies on the smoker initiating the calls; proactive support involves the counsellor initiating the calls to the client, usually at prearranged times. Proactive telephone counselling can also increase the frequency of calls at times when the risk of relapse is at its greatest (that is, the first few days and weeks of a quit attempt) (Zhu, 2005). Adding **proactive telephone counselling** to a minimal intervention, compared to minimal intervention alone, **increases long-term abstinence rates** by approximately 50% (OR = 1.56) (Stead et al., 2004).

Telephone counselling usually focuses on boosting motivation to make a quit attempt, reinforcing the 'not-even-one-puff' message, advising on withdrawal symptoms and medication use, as well as answering any questions.

5.2.2 Combined telephone and face-to-face counselling

Adding telephone support to face-to-face counselling, to further increase the chances of continued abstinence, is a seemingly logical approach. However, currently there is **no evidence** to support this approach (Stead et al., 2004).

Despite this lack of evidence, there are situations where proactive telephone counselling is indicated. When the intensity of face-to-face counselling is low, for example a single session for hospital in-patients, then providing additional telephone counselling has been shown to have a positive effect (for example Miller et al., 1997). This may be a practical approach to take in other situations where smokers cannot attend more than a single, face-to-face counselling session, although it is worth noting that a single call after discharge is unlikely to be effective, and a series of support calls will be required (Miller et al., 1997).

5.2.3 Telephone follow-ups to treatment

To date there is **no evidence** that telephone follow-up following intensive treatment reduces relapse rates (Hajek et al., 2005). However, **ongoing telephone contact** can **identify clients that have relapsed** (these clients can then be supported in making another quit attempt), and may **reduce** the number of people that are **lost to follow-up** when smoking cessation outcome is measured (usually at six or twelve months) (see Section 4.1 Smoking cessation treatments and their outcomes).

5.3 Multiple choice questions

Question 1: The most common source of referral to the Stop Smoking Services is:

a GPs

b Practice nurses

c Pharmacists

d Hospital consultants

e Self-referral

Question 2: Regarding telephone counselling, which of the following statements is TRUE?

a Achieves higher success rates than face-to-face counselling

b Reactive telephone counselling is the most effective method

c Proactive telephone counselling involves the client initiating the calls

d Adding proactive telephone counselling to intensive face-to-face support increases success rates by 50%

e Adding proactive telephone counselling to an intervention that has minimal face-to-face support has been shown to increase success rate

References

Adams, J., Beach, J., Carter, C., Fitchett, A. & Jones, S. (2005). Evaluation of drop-in to quit. Poster presentation, 1st UK National Smoking Cessation Conference, 9 & 10 June 2005, London.

Hajek, P., Stead, L.F., West, R., Jarvis, M. & Lancaster, T. (2005). Relapse prevention interventions for smoking cessation. *The Cochrane Database of Systematic Reviews*, Issue 1. Art. No.: CD003999. DOI: 10.1002/14651858.CD003999.pub2.

Health Development Agency (2002). *Standard for Training in Smoking Cessation Treatments*. London: Health Development Agency.

Johnstone, K. (2005). Evening smoking cessation drop-in clinics (aimed at smokers on low incomes). Poster presentation, 1st UK National Smoking Cessation Conference, 9 & 10 June 2005, London.

Judge, K., Bauld, L., Chesterman, J. & Ferguson, J. (2005). The English Smoking Treatment Services: short-term outcomes. *Addiction*, *100* (Suppl. 2), 46–58.

Miller, N.H., Smith, P.M., DeBusk, R.F., Sobel, D.S. & Taylor, C.B. (1997). Smoking cessation in hospitalised patients. Results of a randomised trial. *Archives of Internal Medicine* 24 Feb., *157* (4), 409–415.

Stead, L.F., Lancaster, T. & Perera, R. (2004). Telephone counselling for smoking cessation. *Cochrane Database of Systematic Reviews*, (4), CD002850.

Zhu, S.-H. (2005). Telephone quitlines: evidence and promise. Oral presentation, 1st UK National Smoking Cessation Conference, 9 & 10 June 2005, London.

Chapter 6
Group interventions

This chapter is aimed at health professionals who provide treatment for smokers in groups; they will probably work as full-time advisers within NHS Stop Smoking Services and will certainly have attended a specialist training course (HDA, 2002). It is anticipated that health professionals intending to deliver group interventions to smokers will have a thorough understanding of the information in Part One (Chapters 1 and 2) of this manual. It is also expected that they will have the knowledge and skills required to deliver brief advice (Chapter 3) and one-to-one treatment (Chapter 4). This chapter involves adapting the contents of Chapter 4 to make it appropriate for group settings, describes some specific additional features of group treatment and makes administrative and logistic recommendations. Box 6.1 explains some of the reasons for treating smokers in groups.

6.1 Recruitment and assessment

Although group treatment has advantages over individual treatment, it is only possible to run groups where there are enough smokers to treat, otherwise it takes too long to accumulate enough smokers for reasonably sized groups (West et al., 2003).

6.1.1 Recruiting for groups

While many clinics run large and successful groups, others claim that it is difficult to recruit smokers to anything other than individual sessions. Given the choice, **clients** generally show a **preference for one-to-one** treatment, although the way **group treatment is presented** can be important. Echoes of 'counselling' or 'group therapy' seem generally off-putting, whereas when group treatment is presented

Box 6.1 Rationale for treating smokers in groups.

Treatment effects
There are no research studies directly comparing group and individual treatments as currently practiced, but there is some indirect evidence that groups may be slightly more effective (Hajek et al., 1985). Studies of pharmacological treatments on similar populations show higher success rates for those treated in groups compared with those treated individually (see Stead & Lancaster, 2000). Within NHS Stop Smoking Services, groups produce higher success rates than individual treatments (Judge et al., 2005; McEwen et al., 2006). Such results could be due to differences in therapists or populations treated, but they do suggest that groups are not an inferior option.

Cost efficacy
In about the same time that it would take to see two individual smokers, a group of approximately 20 smokers can be treated. As group treatment is at least as effective as individual treatment, this means that groups can be ten times more cost effective. Or, to put it differently, if you are providing treatment in groups and have only a limited amount of time at your disposal, you can help ten times as many people in this time than if you treated them individually. (See Parrott et al., 1998; West et al., 2000)

Therapist considerations
Where therapists treat large numbers of smokers, individual treatment can become repetitive and treatment 'failures' can knock their confidence. Groups, on the other hand, generate substantial interest and enthusiasm and the focus is always on those clients maintaining abstinence and not those who continue to smoke.

Box 6.2 Advertising of treatment.

The **advertising** of treatment to smokers is not covered in this manual, although simple advertising methods appear obvious: posters, leaflets, referral cards, training, or local media features. There have been calls for a more strategic approach to the marketing of NHS Stop Smoking Services (Hastings, 2005) and recent NHS advertising campaigns have begun to prompt viewers to call the NHS Smoking Helpline. Section 5.1 (Recruiting smokers into treatment by telephone) covers the main aspects of recruitment, including what to say to clients when they first contact NHS Stop Smoking Services.

simply as 'smokers clinic' or 'group course' this seems to generate little resistance. Box 6.2 discusses advertising of treatment.

To run groups, a list of **potential clients** needs to be generated over a relatively **short time period**. This is normally only possible for **NHS Stop Smoking Clinics** with a large catchment area. Health professionals with a smaller pool of potential clients (for example community pharmacists or practice nurses in smaller practices) cannot normally hope to run groups without having clients on their waiting list for months. This also means that groups are not feasible for any particular subgroup, such as pregnant smokers, as no service has enough of such clients at any given time.

What sort of treatment method do you use to help smokers quit?	*We use a method called withdrawal oriented treatment. This combines intensive support with medications, such as Zyban or NRT, to help you quit. The treatment focuses on helping you to get through the most difficult first few weeks of the quit attempt.*

6.1.2 Assessing clients for group treatment

Following initial contact from smokers, normally by telephone, the usual practice is to invite smokers to an **initial assessment** and information group session (preparation session, see Section 4.4.1); and to start this with brief individual screening. Although the **vast majority** of smokers are perfectly **suitable for group treatment**, there are a **few exceptions** where individual treatment is a better option (see Table 6.1). The initial telephone contact and/or the individual screening at the first group treatment session (to process questionnaires, take CO readings and answer questions) provide an opportunity to assess suitability for group treatment.

Table 6.1 Reasons why some clients are more suitable for one-to-one treatment.

Reason for not attending groups	Examples	Benefits of individual treatment
Client cannot attend at same time and day each week	Shift workers Carers	The timing of one-to-one treatment sessions can be more flexible
Client may be disruptive and/or their behaviour could lead to them being ostracised	Acute mental health problems	Client can receive necessary amount of individual attention Mental health worker may also be able to be present
Client fearful of group treatment	Degree of social phobia	Client can receive individual treatment in a 'less threatening' environment
Client cannot physically attend central clinic	Mobility problems Agoraphobia	One-to-one treatment may be offered at client's home
Client cannot communicate fully within group settings	Impaired hearing Non-English speaking	Client and adviser can be assisted with communication by an interpreter/signer

6.1.3 Logistics of group treatment

As a rule of thumb, only about **half** to **two-thirds of smokers** who say they will attend the first group session will actually **turn up**, although attendance may be improved by shorter waiting times. Smokers usually receive a letter containing a brief explanation of what the **treatment will involve**, the **time** and **date** of the preparation group, a list of dates of the **remaining sessions** and **directions** to the clinic. Clinics, where group treatment is held, do best if they are easily accessible and at attractive locations. Large hospitals tend to be good venues as they have a certain prestige, people know where they are and they have good public transport links.

Running effective group treatment requires particular experience and skills, and is usually best undertaken by core staff employed as smoking specialists. Although **groups** can be run by a single person they are more often **run by two advisers**. With two advisers there is less risk of a group being cancelled if one cannot attend and, with evening groups especially, there is a safety issue. Two advisers can also share the work of individual screening at the first group (CO readings, setting up the room, dispensing medication); in fact some services have additional advisers at these sessions to minimise the amount of time spent on screening and so reduce the waiting time for group participants before treatment begins.

6.2 Treatment programme for groups

There are two main approaches to treating smokers in groups. One is didactic ('**therapist-oriented**') with the adviser as teacher and the group as class. The main objective is to **impart information** on how to achieve and maintain abstinence from smoking. The other focuses primarily on mutual support among group members ('**group-oriented**'). The core function of this approach is to use **group processes** to generate **determination** and **support** to achieve abstinence. In practice, most groups combine these two elements, but with a different balance.

Groups are normally '**closed**', in that clients start treatment together and, for those that remain, 'graduate' together when the group finishes. The present chapter concerns the content and processes of closed groups. There is an option to run **open groups**, which mix smokers in different stages of the quitting process, but this makes the provision of information and work with group processes difficult. These 'drop-in' or 'rolling' groups provide some support and encouragement and can provide a useful community based option for smokers.

What happens at the group sessions?

The advisers provide the same guidance and medication you would get in individual treatment, but groups also provide an opportunity to compare notes with other people going through the same thing as you. This contact with other smokers can give group members valuable support through the first few weeks and an extra reason to stick with their decision not to smoke.

6.3 Group treatment content

The content of **group treatment** does **not differ** greatly from the content of **one-to-one treatment** as described in Chapter 4 (see especially Section 4.4 Behavioural support - withdrawal oriented treatment). The following sections will highlight any significant changes in content, but will mainly focus on how to deliver this treatment to groups.

6.3.1 Preparation

See Section 4.4.1 Preparation.

This first group session with smokers is primarily about **providing information** about what is on offer so that they can make up their minds on whether they would like to take part or not. It will also include **guidance** on what **medication** to use and how to obtain it. The advisers explain **how** the **treatment works** and what is going to happen at the sessions. They provide **accurate information** about **what to expect** during the quit attempt and how to **deal with difficult situations**. The appointment will probably last up to two hours, including the initial individual screening, and will usually take place one week before the quit date. Some services have an additional pre-quit session to allow clients to take their bupropion for 8–14 days prior to quitting. In this session, the focus is on helping clients to get to know each other, reinforcing clients' commitment to the target quit date and discussing preparation for it.

I feel a little afraid of groups, what else can you offer me?	*Don't worry, lots of people feel like this at first and if necessary we can always offer you an individual treatment session. If you can it is best to see what the first group session is like. Most people enjoy the experience of quitting with other smokers, but if it is not for you we can arrange to see you individually.*

It facilitates group interaction if clients can **address each other by name**. Group participants and advisers can write their first name with a thick felt-tip pen in large letters on A4 paper and put these on the floor in front of them at the first session. These name tags can then be re-used over the life-span of the group. The box below gives an example of explaining group treatment.

In the first couple of weeks, at the preparation and quit sessions, there is a lot of information to get through and this may mean that the advisers are doing a lot of the talking. However, this is your quit attempt and many of you here will have made previous attempts to stop smoking – so it is not only the advisers who can contribute to discussions on preparing to quit, choice and use of medication, the quit date, withdrawal symptoms and how to deal with difficult situations. ”

The main 'active ingredient' in groups for smokers is thought to be the **effect of group membership on motivation** to maintain abstinence. Smokers quitting on their own can abort the quit attempt fairly easily, whereas quitting with a group brings along a much stronger commitment. This commitment or '**group effect**' can be created by a combination of processes: a feeling of **responsibility** (for example not wanting to let the group/buddy down), **competition** ('if they can do it, I can do it'), fear of **embarrassment** (for example not wanting to be 'the weakest link'), **encouragement** (for example seeing others achieve and maintain abstinence), the effects of **praise** (for example congratulations and approval from the group for not smoking) and **group pressure**.

The advisers can focus on these '**group effects**' by **facilitating interaction** among group members so that they get to know each other and the group becomes a relevant social forum, and by **special interventions** aimed at facilitating the relevant processes (see 'buddying', 'betting', and 'end of session promises' in Section 6.3.2 Quit date). In groups, as in individual treatment, an adviser's personal style and communication skills can be important. Apart from the basics covered in the chapter on individual treatment, group advisers need to be reasonably confident and relaxed in social situations, to feel comfortable running a group, and also able to step back from the 'teacher' role to allow group interaction without unnecessary interventions. The box below gives an example of explaining group treatment.

As advisers we have run a number of groups like this, but each one is different, because the people in them are different, and what they experience during their quit attempt is different too. The one thing that is the same for all of you is that you will be going through this at the same time, so you will be able to share your experiences, learn from the experiences of others and support each other through this.

Group members will be advised that their last cigarette will be the one immediately before the quit date group; they could be encouraged to smoke these together.

In these groups, do people have to talk about their life problems or their childhood?

No. Stop smoking treatment is not psychotherapy. These sessions are more like evening classes where people come to learn together as a group about stopping smoking.

6.3.2 Quit date

See Section 4.4.2 Quit date.

The quit date group may start with a 'ceremonial' dumping of any remaining cigarettes, lighters and ashtrays. It will include clients trying NRT and a discussion of this and other aspects of NRT, as with individual treatment. Similarly, for those clients using bupropion there will be a discussion about usage and any side effects. Ensuring that clients have an accurate perception of what the medications can and cannot offer is important to establish at this stage. The following box gives an example of explaining medication effectiveness and use.

Both Zyban and NRT, if used properly, are effective in helping smokers to quit, but they are not magic cures. A successful quit attempt needs proper use of medication, but it will also need all the determination you can muster. Although the medications definitely help, they do not make quitting effortless.

As in individual treatment, there is also a discussion of the **importance** of getting through the **first critical week** without smoking, and a discussion of coping strategies. Therapist-oriented advisers tend to present behavioural advice; group-oriented advisers encourage **group discussion**, with participants **learning from each other's past experience**.

In addition to this, the group provides an opportunity to activate **social support** to reinforce clients' determination to remain abstinent over the following week. Typically, clients are paired and the pair members (**buddies**) are instructed on phoning each other daily. The pairs may also be invited to deposit small amounts of money with the return of the deposit contingent on both buddies remaining abstinent. The session may conclude with the clients making a **public promise** that they **will not smoke** over the following week.

Box 6.3 Co-morbidity.

Co-morbidity just means that the client is suffering from two (or more) health conditions – in this case dependence on cigarettes plus one other. Where co-morbid conditions act against clients participating in groups then they should be offered one-to-one treatment (see Section 6.1.2 Assessing clients for group treatment).

It is likely that there will be clients within groups who are suffering from, often serious, smoking-related conditions (coronary heart disease, COPD and even cancer). There is a balance for the advisers to strike in recognising the importance of these conditions to those individuals, and not allowing this to dominate proceedings of the group.

What happens to people who say they will not smoke, but do?

The other people in the group are usually very supportive and, together with the advisers, will try to help the person to get back on track and to catch up with the rest of the group.

6.3.3 Post-quit groups

See Section 4.4.4 Post-quit sessions.

The remaining group sessions normally consist of clients reporting on **how their week went**; and planning for challenges of the **week ahead.** The advisers may prompt them, if needed, to report on their **medication use** and **supply, support** received and needed (including buddy contacts), **difficulties** encountered and **lessons learned.** Groups are normally chatty, humorous and lively. With very 'active' groups the advisers need to make sure that **each client** has the opportunity to **discuss how their week has gone.**

In group-oriented groups, the **advisers** try to **step in only** if some essential technical **information is needed** (for example on medication use, or the likely duration of a particular withdrawal symptom). The focus remains primarily on facilitating 'free' group discussion. In therapist-oriented groups, advisers would provide a more structured input, along the lines of one-to-one treatment. The box below gives an example of **stimulating discussion of individual experiences.**

Some of you will have had a harder time of it than others this past week, and sometimes that is just the way it is. It is worth discussing how different people have coped with their urges to smoke.

Sessions are normally concluded with **renewed promises** of **not smoking** over the next week.

Box 6.4 Difficult group members.

Groups usually contain several extrovert and well-balanced individuals who set the tone, and one of the highlights of smokers' groups is their unproblematic and supportive atmosphere. Shy and silent members rarely pose a problem. Those with severe social phobia should be seen individually, and those with moderate anxiety in social situations are normally easily accommodated by the group.

The one challenge for group advisers is an occasional 'over-talkative' group member. If one person monopolises the initial session, the advisers can approach them afterwards and explain that although their contribution is valuable, they also need to allow time for the contribution of others. At the next session one adviser may want to sit next to them and, if needed, gently remind them of this. If a 'subgroup' develops, with two or three people chatting, the advisers can interrupt them and ask for one person to talk at a time so the rest of the group does not miss out.

What happens after the group sessions have finished?	*If you make it to the end of treatment without smoking then you will be well on your way to being a long-term ex-smoker. The likelihood is that you will not need much more support. However, if you do you are always welcome to get in touch with me.*

6.3.4 End of treatment, relapse prevention and ongoing support

See Section 4.4.5 End of treatment and relapse prevention.

At the last group session clients often express concern that staying abstinent will become harder now that they no longer have the support of the group. Reassurance is provided (as in individual treatment) regarding continued **medication** use; **contact** with 'buddies', other group members and with the advisers if needed; and any 'relapse prevention' sessions or **ongoing support** that the service offers. An example of discussing end-of-group treatment is shown in the box below.

In these first four weeks after your quit date you all managed not to smoke because of your motivation not to do so, because of the medication that you used and because of the support that you got from this group and from elsewhere. It is now time to move into the second phase of your quit attempt where you continue to be motivated and to use your medication, but you get the support you need, which is probably less than you needed in the first couple of weeks, from outside this group. Eventually, of course, in another month or two, you will most likely stop using your medication as well.

There will be discussion and advice on identifying, and avoiding or coping with, potential relapse situations. 'Buddies' can be encouraged to remain in contact and the whole group can be encouraged to carry on meeting (for example at the same day and the same time at the nearest pub). Experience suggests that although group members are usually enthusiastic about continuing to meet up, 'self-help' meetings rarely last longer than a week or two. If necessary, the advisers can be more didactic at this session than previously, without concern over disrupting group interactions.

Appendix 4 lists smoking cessation resources that smokers can use for obtaining ongoing support.

6.4 Monitoring and follow-up

Aspects of monitoring, including the collection of routine and additional data, have been covered in Chapter 4 (Section 4.5 Monitoring). If your service contacts all clients, or a sample of clients, to follow up on their progress at 12 months (or three, six and nine months as some services do) then clients should be informed of this at the last group.

6.4.1 Record keeping

The Russell Standard (Clinical) described in Chapter 4 (Section 4.1.2 Short-term treatment outcomes) is, of course, as applicable to group treatment as it is to one-to-one treatment. The difference with group treatment is purely one of logistics because of the numbers of clients involved.

6.5 Multiple choice questions

Question 1: Regarding group treatment, which of the following statements is FALSE?

- **a** There are no studies directly comparing group with individual treatment as currently practiced
- **b** There is no evidence that groups might be more effective than individual treatment
- **c** To be sustainable group treatment generally requires a local population of 200 000 people
- **d** Groups may not be practicable in settings with small catchment areas
- **e** Groups are more cost effective than individual treatment

Question 2: Which of the following is NOT a reason for suggesting that individual treatment might be more suitable than group treatment?

- **a** The client is going to miss the second follow-up session
- **b** The client cannot attend three of the sessions
- **c** The client has hearing difficulties
- **d** The client is fearful of groups
- **e** The client has acute mental health problems

Question 3: What percentage of clients invited to the first group session can be expected to actually turn up?

- **a** 0–20%
- **b** 20–40%
- **c** 40–60%
- **d** 60–80%
- **e** 80–100%

Question 4: At the information session, which of the following tasks is NOT undertaken?

- **a** Clients have carbon monoxide measured in their breath
- **b** Clients are given accurate and positive expectations
- **c** Client are informed that approximately 60% of them will be abstinent at the end of treatment
- **d** Clients are given guidance on NRT
- **e** Clients are advised to set a quit date even if they are not sure about quitting

Question 5: On the quit day, which of the following tasks is NOT undertaken?

- **a** Clients try NRT
- **b** The importance of a good start is discussed
- **c** There is a discussion of how to cope with urges to smoke and difficult situations
- **d** Clients are instructed on how to keep a smoking diary
- **e** Buddies place a bet with each other to increase commitment not to smoke

Question 6: On the post-quit sessions, which of the following tasks is NOT undertaken?

- **a** Clients discuss how their week has been
- **b** Clients that have had a lapse are advised not to return to the group
- **c** Medication use is discussed
- **d** There is a discussion of how to cope with urges to smoke and difficult situations
- **e** Clients renew their promises that they won't smoke to the group

References

Hajek, P., Belcher, M. & Stapleton, J. (1985). Enhancing the impact of groups: an evaluation of two group formats for smokers. *British Journal of Clinical Psychology*, *24*, 289–294.

Hastings, G. (2005). Marketing cessation services: loyalty, relationships and customer service. Oral presentation, 1st UK National Smoking Cessation Conference, 9 & 10 June 2005, London.

Health Development Agency (2002). *Standard for Training in Smoking Cessation Treatments*. London: Health Development Agency.

Judge, K., Bauld, L., Chesterman, J. & Ferguson, J. (2005). The English Smoking Treatment Services: short-term outcomes. *Addiction, 100* (Suppl. 2), 46–58.

McEwen, A., West, R. & McRobbie, H. (2006). Effectiveness of specialist group treatment for smoking cessation vs one-to-one treatment in primary care. *Addictive Behaviours*. In press.

Parrott, S., Godfrey, C., Raw, M., West, R. & McNeill, A. (1998). Guidance for commissioners on the cost effectiveness of smoking cessation interventions. *Thorax, 53* (Suppl. 5 Pt 2), S1–38.

Stead, L.F. & Lancaster, T. (2000). Group behaviour therapy programmes for smoking cessation. *Cochrane Database of Systematic Reviews, 2*, CD001007.

West, R., McNeill, A. & Raw, M. (2000). National smoking cessation guidelines for health professionals: an update. *Thorax, 55*, 987–999.

West, R., McNeill, A. & Raw, M. (2003). *Meeting Department of Health Smoking Cessation Targets: Recommendations for Primary Care Trusts and Practitioners*. London: Health Development Agency.

Answers to multiple choice questions

The answers to the questions relating to smoking patterns and prevalence were correct at time of going to press, but of course these items will change over time.

Chapter 1: Smoking demographics

Question: 1 = c, 2 = b, 3 = c, 4 = c, 5 = b, 6 = b, 7 = b, 8 = b, 9 = d, 10 = a, 11 = e, 12 = c.

Chapter 2: The health risks of smoking and the benefits of stopping

Question: 1 = c, 2 = e, 3 = d, 4 = d, 5 = b, 6 = a, 7 = d, 8 = a, 9 = d, 10 = b, 11 = c, 12 = a.

Chapter 3: Brief interventions

Question: 1 = a, 2 = c, 3 = d, 4 = e, 5 = a, 6 = e, 7 = d, 8 = b, 9 = a, 10 = c, 11 = c, 12 = d, 13 = b, 14 = e, 15 = d, 16 = c, 17 = b, 18 = c, 19 = c, 20 = e.

Chapter 4: Intensive one to one support and advice

Question: 1 = e, 2 = c, 3 = e, 4 = c, 5 = c, 6 = c, 7 = e, 8 = b, 9 = c, 10 = a, 11 = b, 12 = a, 13 = b, 14 = c, 15 = a, 16 = e, 17 = b, 18 = e, 19 = b, 20 = d, 21 = c, 22 = a, 23 = e, 24 = d, 25 = a, 26 = c.

Chapter 5: Telephone counselling

Question: 1 = e, 2 = e.

Chapter 6: Group interventions

Question: 1 = b, 2 = a, 3 = c, 4 = e, 5 = d, 6 = b.

Appendix 1

Bupropion (Zyban) – special patient groups

Patient type	Recommendation
Children and adolescents	Not recommended in patients under 18yrs of age – no data available.
Elderly	Use with caution. Increased sensitivity may be an issue (more likely to have decreased renal function); 150 mg once daily is recommended.
Hepatically impaired	Contraindicated in patients with severe hepatic cirrhosis (reduced clearance leading to high plasma levels). Use with caution in mild-to-moderate hepatic impairment, which may lead to higher levels; 150 mg daily is recommended. Monitor closely for possible undesirable effects (e.g. insomnia, dry mouth, seizures) indicating high drug metabolite levels.
Renally impaired	Use with caution; 150 mg once daily recommended. Monitor closely for possible undesirable effects (e.g. insomnia, dry mouth, seizures) indicating high drug metabolite levels.
Psychiatric	Contraindicated in patients with a history of bipolar disorder. May precipitate psychotic episodes in susceptible patients; use with caution.
Pregnant or lactating women	Zyban must not be used in pregnancy/lactation, no data is available on this patient group, risk unknown. If pharmacotherapy is required consider NRT, which is also contraindicated in some products, but safer than smoking in pregnancy.
Predisposed towards seizure	Contraindicated in patients with current or previous seizure disorder. Use with extreme caution in patients with certain conditions including: ■ History of brain trauma ■ Brain injury ■ Concomitant administration of medicines known to lower the seizure threshold e.g. antipsychotics, antidepressants such as SSRIs, theophylline, systemic steroids

Patient type	Recommendation
	Also use with caution in circumstances of: ■ Alcohol abuse ■ Abrupt withdrawal from alcohol/benzodiazepines ■ Diabetes treated with hypoglycaemics/insulin (reduce dose to 150 mg per day) ■ Use of stimulants/anorectic products
Eating disorders	Contraindicated in patients with current or previous diagnosis of bulimia or anorexia nervosa.
Sensitivity	Contraindicated in patients with current hypersensitivity to Zyban or excipients in the tablets (excipients do not include lactose). Discontinue if patient experiences hypersensitivity or anaphylactic reactions, e.g. rash, pruritis, urticaria, chest pain, oedema or dyspnoea.

Appendix 2

Bupropion (Zyban) – drug interactions

Interaction	Examples	Recommended action
MAOIs	Tranylcypromine Phenelzine Moclobemide	Contraindicated. At least 14 days should elapse between discontinuation of irreversible MAOIs and initiation of Zyban.
Drugs metabolised by the CYP2D6 enzyme (a subset of the hepatic metabolic enzyme system cytochrome p450)	Antidepressants e.g. desipramine, imipramine, paroxetine Antipsychotics e.g. thioridazine, risperidone Beta-blockers e.g. metoprolol Type 1c antiarrhythmics e.g. flecainide propafenone	Initiate concomitant therapy at the lower end of the dosage range or decrease dose when Zyban added to the treatment regimen.
Drugs metabolised by CYPA2	Theophylline Clozapine	Administer with caution.
Drugs that lower seizure threshold	Antipsychotics Antidepressants Theophylline Systemic steroids Abrupt discontinuation of benzodiazepines Quinolones (e.g. Ciprofloxacin)	Administer with extreme caution.
Drugs which may inhibit the metabolism of Zyban	Cimetidine Sodium valproate	Administer with caution. Reduce dose to 150 mg per day.
Drugs which may induce the metabolism of Zyban	Carbamazepine Phenobarbitone Phenytoin	Administer with caution. Zyban is contraindicated in patients with current or previous seizure disorder.

Interaction	Examples	Recommended action
Drugs which may affect Zyban's metabolism by the CYP2B6 isoenzyme	Orphenadrine Cyclophosphamide Ifosfamide	Administer with caution.
Other important interactions	Levodopa	Administer with caution.

Appendix 3

Effect of tobacco abstinence on metabolism of some drugs

Tobacco smoking increases the metabolism of theophylline; smoking cessation can cause theophylline plasma levels to rise. Clients taking theophylline should be advised to consult with their GP about stopping smoking. Smoking cessation may also cause alterations in the circulating drug levels of the following (but not normally enough to cause therapeutic problems):

- Insulin
- Adrenergic agonists and antagonists
- Flecainide
- Tacrine

Clients who are taking any of the above medication should be advised to inform their GP that they are trying to stop smoking.

From the NRT PGD, PharmacyHealthLink website:
www.pharmacyhealthlink.org.uk

Abstinence increases levels of the following drugs:

- Clomipramine
- Clozapine
- Desipramine
- Desmethyldiazepam
- Doxepin
- Fluphenazine
- Haloperidol

- Imipramine
- Oxazepam

Abstinence does not alter the levels of the following drugs:

- Amitriptyline
- Ethanol
- Lorazepam
- Midazolam
- Triazolam

Effects of abstinence on the levels of the following drugs are unclear:

- Alprazolam
- Chlorpromazine
- Diazepam
- Nortriptyline

From: Hughes, J. (1993). Effects of smoke-free in-patient units on psychiatric diagnosis and treatment. *Journal of Clinical Psychiatry*, *54*, 109–114.

Appendix 4

Resources

Smoking cessation resources for smokers trying to stop and for health professionals assisting in these quit attempts.

Stop smoking resources for clients

The Stop Smoking Handbook by Andy McEwen, Hayden McRobbie & Andrew Preston	Comprehensive information for people stopping smoking or contemplating stopping smoking. Available from the publishers. Tel. 01305 262244.
NHS Stop Smoking website	NHS website offering information, advice and support, and a link to find a local NHS Stop Smoking Service (www.givingupsmoking.co.uk).
NHS Smoking Helpline	Help and advice to quit by telephone (0800 169 0 169).
QUIT	Expert assistance to quit by telephone (0800 0022 00) or online (www.quit.org.uk).
No Smoking Day	Charity providing help to smokers wanting to quit on No Smoking Day (www.nosmokingday.org.uk).
Nicorette	Pfizer website with details of all their Nicorette NRT products plus information on Cut Down To Stop (www.nicorette.co.uk).
Click2Quit	A GSK website offering their 'Committed Quitters' package of tailored support (www.Click2Quit.com). See also www.thetimeisright.com a website offering

	information and support for quitters plus information on their NRT products.
Nicotinell	Nicotinell website offering an online support programme and information about their NRT products (www.nicotinell.com).

Stop smoking resources for health professionals

Smoking Cessation Services Research Network (SCSRN)	The best one-stop website for clinical, research and policy resources (www.scsrn.org).
UK National Smoking Cessation Conference (UKNSCC)	An annual conference to assist the professional development of the field. The conference website has a permanent free archive of conference abstracts, presentation notes, powerpoint presentations and delegate reports (www.uknscc.org).
Smoking Cessation Training and Research programme (SCTRP) Update and Supervision Day	An annual update on treatment and service developments, with an opportunity for clinical supervision for graduates of SCTRP courses (sctrp@yahoo.co.uk).
Smoking cessation: Fast facts by Robert West & Saul Shiffman	Published in 2004 by Health Press Limited this book gives practical advice for interventions, along with current information about the effects of smoking, the consequences of smoking cessation and the myths about smoking and quitting (www.healthpress.co.uk).
Action on Smoking and Health (ASH)	ASH is a campaigning public health charity and their website provides useful facts on smoking and health, the tobacco industry and quitting smoking (www.ash.org.uk). ASH has regional branches, and national branches in Wales and Northern Ireland.
Action on Smoking and Health (ASH) Scotland	ASH Scotland is the leading voluntary organisation campaigning for effective tobacco control legislation in Scotland (www.ashscotland.org.uk).

QUIT	In addition to telephone and online support for quitters, QUIT offers training courses for health professionals (0207 251 1551) (www.quit.org.uk).
No Smoking Day	Charity providing promotional materials and support for health professionals wanting to organise activities for No Smoking Day (www.nosmokingday.org.uk).
Cochrane Library	Systematic reviews of smoking cessation interventions (www.cochrane.org).
PharmacyHealthLink	A charity that promotes health through pharmacy and also contains templates of Patient Group Directions for NRT and bupropion (www.pharmacyhealthlink.org.uk).
Globalink	Discussion forum for smoking cessation and tobacco control (www.globalink.org). Any health professional involved in smoking cessation should sign up for the UK discussion list.
Office for National Statistics (ONS)	Government website acting as the home of official UK statistics (www.statistics.gov.uk).
Society for Research on Nicotine & Tobacco (SRNT)	An international scientific organisation dedicated to research on tobacco use (www.srnt.org).
Treat Tobacco	A website for evidence-based smoking cessation information (www.treatobacco.net).
Bedfont Ltd	Website of one of the manufacturers of CO monitors (www.bedfont.com).
Micro Medical Ltd	Website of one of the manufacturers of CO monitors (www.micromedical.co.uk).

Training for health professionals

The Smoking Cessation Training and Research Programme (SCTRP) was the first course offering training for health professionals in smoking cessation and it remains the most popular training course of its kind. Contact email address: sctrp@yahoo.co.uk

There are a number of other training courses that also provide training for those who want to deliver smoking cessation treatment as part of NHS Stop Smoking Services. There is no register of training courses but a survey was carried out in 2001 and this report is available on the Research Reviews page of the Smoking Cessation Services Research Network (SCSRN) website: www.scsrn.org

Appendix 5

Examples of what to say when intervening with smoking clients

Below are two suggestions of how to ask about **smoking status**. The opening one is for when a **client** is seen for the **first time** (for example when a patient registers with a GP practice) and the second for **existing clients** (for example during a regular consultation or follow-up appointment).

Do you smoke cigarettes or tobacco at all, or have you ever smoked regularly?

Are you still smoking/not smoking?

The next boxes are examples of, first, **how to respond** when a client reports being a **non-smoker** and, second, when they report being an **ex-smoker**.

Well done for not smoking. As you probably know smoking is one of the most harmful things that you can do.

Well done for not smoking. Staying an ex-smoker will mean a lot for your future health.

The next five statements provide a variety of ways in which smoking clients can be **advised to stop**.

You probably already know the risks involved with smoking, but I cannot stress enough how important it is to stop. It is the best thing that you can do to improve your health.

The best thing you can do for your health is to stop smoking, and I would advise you to stop as soon as possible.

Quitting smoking will substantially decrease the risk of you developing cancer, heart disease and lung disease. You could also save a lot of money – a 20-a-day smoker will save at least £1500 per year.

Most smokers want to give up smoking at some point. You might want to think about stopping smoking sooner rather than later.

As your doctor/nurse/pharmacist/name of health profession it is my duty to advise you to stop smoking. Stopping smoking is the single best thing that you can do to improve your current and future health.

These four phrases provide suggested ways of **assessing** how **interested** clients are in **stopping smoking** and in receiving help to stop.

If you would like to give up smoking I can help you.

If you are interested in stopping smoking there are services and medications which can help you in your quit attempt. Would you be interested in stopping smoking?

Tobacco is very addictive, so it can be very difficult to give up, and many people have to try several times before they succeed. Your chances of succeeding are much greater if you make use of counselling support, which I can arrange for you, and either nicotine replacement therapy (NRT) or the drug bupropion (Zyban), which can be prescribed for you.

The NHS provides free and effective treatment for smokers like yourself. In fact you are up to four times more likely to quit using this help than quitting by yourself. Are you interested in such help?

This is one way in which you might like to inform clients about **compensatory smoking**.

It may seem like a good idea to cut down the number of cigarettes that you smoke or to switch to 'lighter' (lower tar) cigarettes – but it is not that simple. Because your mind and body are used to regular doses of nicotine you will ensure that you continue to get similar amounts of nicotine from these fewer, or 'lighter', cigarettes by smoking them more intensely.

Stress relief is one of the main reasons that smokers give for smoking; here is one suggestion of how to dispel the common myth that smoking helps smokers to relax.

Most smokers say that one of the main reasons that they smoke is to help them cope with stress. However, we know that once people stop smoking they are less stressed than when they smoked.

An example of what to say to a smoker about **withdrawal symptoms**.

A smoker's mind and body is used to regular doses of nicotine. When they stop smoking they go through a short period of readjustment where they experience withdrawal symptoms. As long as you do not have even one puff on a cigarette after your quit date these symptoms will gradually get easier to cope with and most will disappear within four weeks.

These next three statements are examples, respectively, of how to explain to clients the **benefits** of receiving **help from NHS Stop Smoking Services**, of **using NRT** and of **using Zyban**.

There is strong evidence that getting help, support and advice in your quit attempt from someone specially trained in smoking cessation will roughly double your chances of success. Medications that help with stopping smoking have a similar effect and our local Stop Smoking Service can help you choose which medication is most suitable for you.

NRT, if used properly, gives you some of the nicotine that you get from cigarettes, but in a different way. NRT helps to reduce the urges to smoke and discomfort (withdrawal symptoms) that smokers experience when they stop smoking, and roughly doubles your chances of staying stopped.

Zyban can reduce the desire to smoke and is taken for at least one week before your quit attempt, in order to build up to therapeutic levels. You will be asked to take one tablet for six days, whilst still smoking, and then increase to two tablets a day. A dry mouth and sleep disturbance are very common side effects, while a small proportion of people suffer more serious side effects such as seizures (fits). Zyban is relatively safe but, because of the side effects, not everyone can take it. If you are one of these people then do not worry as you will be able to use NRT, which is as effective as Zyban and doesn't have any serious side effects.

An example of assessing **client's willingness to attend for treatment**.

I am pleased that you would like to stop smoking and that you would like to see me so that I can help you with this. Regular attendance at appointments is important and so perhaps we can now both check our diaries to make sure that you are able to make the remaining appointments over the next few weeks.

This example of how to respond when a client reveals that they have tried to stop smoking before and failed, aims to **boost** their **motivation**.

I see that you have tried to stop smoking a number of times before and that you have never lasted more than a couple of weeks. Having tried and failed to stop in the past does not harm your chances of quitting successfully this time, and having gone a few weeks without smoking, when the withdrawal symptoms are at their strongest, shows that you can do it.

The first of these two suggested statements explains about carbon monoxide (CO) in cigarette smoke and about the **monitoring of CO levels** during the quit attempt. The second is an example of advising clients about raised CO levels **when they claim that they have not smoked**.

Carbon monoxide (CO) is one of the things that you inhale when you smoke cigarettes; it takes the place of oxygen in your red blood cells and contributes to coronary heart disease. The good news is that if you do not smoke after your quit date then your carbon monoxide levels will drop to that of a non-smoker.

Whilst you are still smoking I would expect your CO levels to be fairly high (depending upon what time of the day we measure your CO), but once you have quit it should drop below 10 ppm. I will measure your CO levels every time I see you with this CO monitor. This will let me know whether you have been smoking and also provide you with a good indication that, however you may be feeling, your health is already improving.

The most common reason for raised CO levels after the quit date is that the person has smoked. However, there are some other possible reasons, such as leaking car exhausts, faulty gas boilers and working with some paint strippers. I would suggest that in the coming week you get your exhaust and gas boiler checked so that when you come back next week, not having smoked, you should have a nice low CO reading.

Clients often have unrealistically high expectations of how medications (NRT and Zyban) can help them stop smoking. The following are suggestions of how to explain the **role medications have in a quit attempt** and their **effectiveness**.

There are two types of medication available to help you in your quit attempt: nicotine replacement therapy (NRT), such as nicotine gum and nicotine patch, and bupropion (Zyban). Both are effective and if used properly will double your chances of stopping smoking. However, they are not a magic cure.

Medications are an important part of a successful quit attempt, but they are not the only part. Receiving professional support and advice from someone like me will also roughly double your chances of stopping smoking, but you will need support from other people too. You will also have to make changes to your daily routine and will have to be highly committed to give yourself a good chance of stopping smoking for good.

Both Zyban and NRT, if used properly, are effective in helping smokers to quit, but they are not magic cures. A successful quit attempt need proper use of medication, but it will also need all the determination you can muster. Although the medications definitely help, they do not make quitting effortless.

Clients are sometimes concerned that the nicotine that they get from NRT will be harmful to them; this is an example of explaining the **safety of NRT**.

Nicotine doesn't cause cancer; it is the tar and carbon monoxide in cigarette smoke that are harmful. NRT will not give you any of the tar and carbon monoxide that you get from cigarettes, but will give you some nicotine to reduce the withdrawal symptoms that many smokers experience when they stop smoking.

The nicotine that you do get from NRT is less than you would get from cigarettes and is absorbed more slowly in the body. This means that very few people use NRT long term, and those that do normally need it. The biggest problem with NRT use is not that people become dependent on the products, it is that people do not use enough of it for long enough.

If Zyban is not suitable for some clients then they need not worry as NRT will still be available to them. Here is an example of explaining **suitability of bupropion** (**Zyban**).

Zyban is an effective medication for helping people to stop smoking. However, because it has certain side effects it is not suitable for all smokers and there are a number of questions that need to be asked to make sure that it is suitable for you. Should this not be the case then there is no need to worry as NRT will be available for use by you and that is equally as effective as Zyban.

This example of debriefing a client who has been **unsuccessful in their quit attempt** encourages clients to learn from their experience and not to be too harsh on themselves; it also leaves the door open for them to seek help from NHS Stop Smoking Services in the future when they want to make another quit attempt.

As you know stopping smoking can be difficult and many smokers need more than one attempt to stop smoking for good. Just because you did not make it this time it does not mean that you will not be successful in the future, and this experience should not deter you from trying again. Hopefully you might have learnt something from this attempt which will put you in a better position next time. The best thing that you can do now is take a break, 'recharge your batteries', and in a few months' time think about preparing to make another attempt at stopping smoking.

Many clients are wary of what group treatment might involve. Below are two examples of **explaining group treatment**.

In the first couple of weeks, at the preparation and quit sessions, there is a lot of information to get through and this may mean that the advisors are doing a lot of the talking. However, this is your quit attempt and many of you here will have made previous attempts to stop smoking, so it is not only the advisors who can contribute to discussions on preparing to quit, choice and use of medication, the quit date, withdrawal symptoms and how to deal with difficult situations.

As advisors we have run a number of groups like this, but each one is different because the people in them are different and what they experience during their quit attempt is different too. The one thing that is the same for all of you is that you will be going through this at the same time, so you will be able to share your experiences, learn from the experiences of others and support each other through this.

An example of how to **stimulate discussion of individual experiences**.

Some of you will have had a harder time of it this past week than others, and sometimes that is just the way it is. It is worth discussing how different people have coped with their urges to smoke.

Clients who have managed not to smoke with the help of group or individual treatment are often anxious about how they will cope without this support. The following is an example of how the **end of treatment** can be explained.

In these first four weeks after your quit date you all managed not to smoke because of your motivation not to do so, because of the medication that you used and because of the support that you got from this group and from elsewhere. It is now time to move into the second phase of your quit attempt where you continue to be motivated and to use your medication, but you get the support you need, which is probably less than you needed in the first couple of weeks, from outside this group. Eventually of course, in another month or two, you will most likely stop using your medication as well.

Index

6330